NOTARY BOOK DETAILS

NOTARY BOOK START DATE:-

NOTARY BOOK END DATE:-

NOTARY LOG BOOK NUMBER:-

PERSONAL INFORMATION

NAME:- _____

ADDRESS:- _____

_____

EMAIL:- _____

PERSONAL NUMBER:- _____

To Whom This Journal Belongs

_____

_____

_____

PERSONAL NOTES

① Notary Public Record

Notarized Date/Time	Date of Document	Type of Documents	Service	Name, Phone #, address of signer	E-mail:
		_____ _____	☐ Acknowledgment ☐ Oath/Affirmation ☐ Jurat ☐ Other _____	_____ _____	Signature

Name, Phone #, address of witness	Signature of witness	Identity	Right Thumbprint	Notary / Travel Fee
		☐ Driver's license ☐ Credible Witness ☐ Passport ☐ Personally Known ☐ I D Card ☐ Other_____ ☐ I D. # _____		

② Notary Public Record

Notarized Date/Time	Date of Document	Type of Documents	Service	Name, Phone #, address of signer	E-mail:
		_____ _____	☐ Acknowledgment ☐ Oath/Affirmation ☐ Jurat ☐ Other _____	_____ _____	Signature

Name, Phone #, address of witness	Signature of witness	Identity	Right Thumbprint	Notary / Travel Fee
		☐ Driver's license ☐ Credible Witness ☐ Passport ☐ Personally Known ☐ I D Card ☐ Other_____ ☐ I D. # _____		

③ Notary Public Record

Notarized Date/Time	Date of Document	Type of Documents	Service	Name, Phone #, address of signer	E-mail:
		_____ _____	☐ Acknowledgment ☐ Oath/Affirmation ☐ Jurat ☐ Other _____	_____ _____	Signature

Name, Phone #, address of witness	Signature of witness	Identity	Right Thumbprint	Notary / Travel Fee
		☐ Driver's license ☐ Credible Witness ☐ Passport ☐ Personally Known ☐ I D Card ☐ Other_____ ☐ I D. # _____		

4   *Notary Public Record*

Notarized Date/Time	Date of Document	Type of Documents	Service	Name, Phone #, address of signer	E-mail:
_____ _____	_____	_____ _____	☐ Acknowledgment ☐ Oath/Affirmation ☐ Jurat ☐ Other _____	_____ _____	Signature _____

Name, Phone #, address of witness	Signature of witness	Identity		Right Thumbprint	Notary / Travel Fee
_____ _____		☐ Driver's license ☐ Credible Witness ☐ Passport ☐ Personally Known ☐ I D Card ☐ Other_____ ☐ I D. # _____			

5   *Notary Public Record*

Notarized Date/Time	Date of Document	Type of Documents	Service	Name, Phone #, address of signer	E-mail:
_____ _____	_____	_____ _____	☐ Acknowledgment ☐ Oath/Affirmation ☐ Jurat ☐ Other _____	_____ _____	Signature _____

Name, Phone #, address of witness	Signature of witness	Identity		Right Thumbprint	Notary / Travel Fee
_____ _____		☐ Driver's license ☐ Credible Witness ☐ Passport ☐ Personally Known ☐ I D Card ☐ Other_____ ☐ I D. # _____			

6   *Notary Public Record*

Notarized Date/Time	Date of Document	Type of Documents	Service	Name, Phone #, address of signer	E-mail:
_____ _____	_____	_____ _____	☐ Acknowledgment ☐ Oath/Affirmation ☐ Jurat ☐ Other _____	_____ _____	Signature _____

Name, Phone #, address of witness	Signature of witness	Identity		Right Thumbprint	Notary / Travel Fee
_____ _____		☐ Driver's license ☐ Credible Witness ☐ Passport ☐ Personally Known ☐ I D Card ☐ Other_____ ☐ I D. # _____			

7 Notary Public Record

Notarized Date/Time	Date of Document	Type of Documents	Service	Name, Phone #, address of signer	E-mail:
			☐ Acknowledgment ☐ Oath/Affirmation ☐ Jurat ☐ Other _____		Signature

Name, Phone #, address of witness	Signature of witness	Identity	Right Thumbprint	Notary / Travel Fee
		☐ Driver's license ☐ Credible Witness ☐ Passport ☐ Personally Known ☐ I D Card ☐ Other_____ ☐ I D. # _____		

8 Notary Public Record

Notarized Date/Time	Date of Document	Type of Documents	Service	Name, Phone #, address of signer	E-mail:
			☐ Acknowledgment ☐ Oath/Affirmation ☐ Jurat ☐ Other _____		Signature

Name, Phone #, address of witness	Signature of witness	Identity	Right Thumbprint	Notary / Travel Fee
		☐ Driver's license ☐ Credible Witness ☐ Passport ☐ Personally Known ☐ I D Card ☐ Other_____ ☐ I D. # _____		

9 Notary Public Record

Notarized Date/Time	Date of Document	Type of Documents	Service	Name, Phone #, address of signer	E-mail:
			☐ Acknowledgment ☐ Oath/Affirmation ☐ Jurat ☐ Other _____		Signature

Name, Phone #, address of witness	Signature of witness	Identity	Right Thumbprint	Notary / Travel Fee
		☐ Driver's license ☐ Credible Witness ☐ Passport ☐ Personally Known ☐ I D Card ☐ Other_____ ☐ I D. # _____		

10 Notary Public Record

Notarized Date/Time	Date of Document	Type of Documents	Service	Name, Phone #, address of signer	E-mail:
			☐ Acknowledgment ☐ Oath/Affirmation ☐ Jurat ☐ Other ————		Signature

Name, Phone #, address of witness	Signature of witness	Identity	Right Thumbprint	Notary / Travel Fee
		☐ Driver's license ☐ Credible Witness ☐ Passport ☐ Personally Known ☐ I D Card ☐ Other_____ ☐ I D. # _____		

11 Notary Public Record

Notarized Date/Time	Date of Document	Type of Documents	Service	Name, Phone #, address of signer	E-mail:
			☐ Acknowledgment ☐ Oath/Affirmation ☐ Jurat ☐ Other ————		Signature

Name, Phone #, address of witness	Signature of witness	Identity	Right Thumbprint	Notary / Travel Fee
		☐ Driver's license ☐ Credible Witness ☐ Passport ☐ Personally Known ☐ I D Card ☐ Other_____ ☐ I D. # _____		

12 Notary Public Record

Notarized Date/Time	Date of Document	Type of Documents	Service	Name, Phone #, address of signer	E-mail:
			☐ Acknowledgment ☐ Oath/Affirmation ☐ Jurat ☐ Other ————		Signature

Name, Phone #, address of witness	Signature of witness	Identity	Right Thumbprint	Notary / Travel Fee
		☐ Driver's license ☐ Credible Witness ☐ Passport ☐ Personally Known ☐ I D Card ☐ Other_____ ☐ I D. # _____		

13 Notary Public Record

Notarized Date/Time	Date of Document	Type of Documents	Service	Name, Phone #, address of signer	E-mail:
		_____	☐ Acknowledgment ☐ Oath/Affirmation ☐ Jurat ☐ Other _____		Signature
_____	_____	_____		_____	
_____		_____		_____	_____

Name, Phone #, address of witness	Signature of witness	Identity	Right Thumbprint	Notary / Travel Fee
_____ _____		☐ Driver's license ☐ Credible Witness ☐ Passport ☐ Personally Known ☐ I D Card ☐ Other_____		
		☐ I D. # _____		

14 Notary Public Record

Notarized Date/Time	Date of Document	Type of Documents	Service	Name, Phone #, address of signer	E-mail:
		_____	☐ Acknowledgment ☐ Oath/Affirmation ☐ Jurat ☐ Other _____		Signature
_____	_____	_____		_____	
_____		_____		_____	_____

Name, Phone #, address of witness	Signature of witness	Identity	Right Thumbprint	Notary / Travel Fee
_____ _____		☐ Driver's license ☐ Credible Witness ☐ Passport ☐ Personally Known ☐ I D Card ☐ Other_____		
		☐ I D. # _____		

15 Notary Public Record

Notarized Date/Time	Date of Document	Type of Documents	Service	Name, Phone #, address of signer	E-mail:
		_____	☐ Acknowledgment ☐ Oath/Affirmation ☐ Jurat ☐ Other _____		Signature
_____	_____	_____		_____	
_____		_____		_____	_____

Name, Phone #, address of witness	Signature of witness	Identity	Right Thumbprint	Notary / Travel Fee
_____ _____		☐ Driver's license ☐ Credible Witness ☐ Passport ☐ Personally Known ☐ I D Card ☐ Other_____		
		☐ I D. # _____		

16 — Notary Public Record

Notarized Date/Time	Date of Document	Type of Documents	Service	Name, Phone #, address of signer	E-mail:
_____ _____	_____	_____	☐ Acknowledgment ☐ Oath/Affirmation ☐ Jurat ☐ Other _____	_____ _____ _____	Signature _____

Name, Phone #, address of witness	Signature of witness	Identity	Right Thumbprint	Notary / Travel Fee
_____ _____	_____	☐ Driver's license ☐ Credible Witness ☐ Passport ☐ Personally Known ☐ I D Card ☐ Other_____ ☐ I D. #_____		

17 — Notary Public Record

Notarized Date/Time	Date of Document	Type of Documents	Service	Name, Phone #, address of signer	E-mail:
_____ _____	_____	_____	☐ Acknowledgment ☐ Oath/Affirmation ☐ Jurat ☐ Other _____	_____ _____ _____	Signature _____

Name, Phone #, address of witness	Signature of witness	Identity	Right Thumbprint	Notary / Travel Fee
_____ _____	_____	☐ Driver's license ☐ Credible Witness ☐ Passport ☐ Personally Known ☐ I D Card ☐ Other_____ ☐ I D. #_____		

18 — Notary Public Record

Notarized Date/Time	Date of Document	Type of Documents	Service	Name, Phone #, address of signer	E-mail:
_____ _____	_____	_____	☐ Acknowledgment ☐ Oath/Affirmation ☐ Jurat ☐ Other _____	_____ _____ _____	Signature _____

Name, Phone #, address of witness	Signature of witness	Identity	Right Thumbprint	Notary / Travel Fee
_____ _____	_____	☐ Driver's license ☐ Credible Witness ☐ Passport ☐ Personally Known ☐ I D Card ☐ Other_____ ☐ I D. #_____		

Notary Public Record

19

Notarized Date/Time	Date of Document	Type of Documents	Service	Name, Phone #, address of signer	E-mail:
		_____	☐ Acknowledgment ☐ Oath/Affirmation ☐ Jurat ☐ Other _____	_____ _____	Signature

Name, Phone #, address of witness	Signature of witness	Identity	Right Thumbprint	Notary / Travel Fee
		☐ Driver's license ☐ Credible Witness ☐ Passport ☐ Personally Known ☐ ID Card ☐ Other_____ ☐ I D. # _____		

Notary Public Record

20

Notarized Date/Time	Date of Document	Type of Documents	Service	Name, Phone #, address of signer	E-mail:
		_____	☐ Acknowledgment ☐ Oath/Affirmation ☐ Jurat ☐ Other _____	_____ _____	Signature

Name, Phone #, address of witness	Signature of witness	Identity	Right Thumbprint	Notary / Travel Fee
		☐ Driver's license ☐ Credible Witness ☐ Passport ☐ Personally Known ☐ I D Card ☐ Other_____ ☐ I D. # _____		

Notary Public Record

21

Notarized Date/Time	Date of Document	Type of Documents	Service	Name, Phone #, address of signer	E-mail:
		_____	☐ Acknowledgment ☐ Oath/Affirmation ☐ Jurat ☐ Other _____	_____ _____	Signature

Name, Phone #, address of witness	Signature of witness	Identity	Right Thumbprint	Notary / Travel Fee
		☐ Driver's license ☐ Credible Witness ☐ Passport ☐ Personally Known ☐ I D Card ☐ Other_____ ☐ I D. # _____		

Notary Public Record

22

Notarized Date/Time	Date of Document	Type of Documents	Service	Name, Phone #, address of signer	E-mail:
			☐ Acknowledgment ☐ Oath/Affirmation ☐ Jurat ☐ Other ————		Signature

Name, Phone #, address of witness	Signature of witness	Identity	Right Thumbprint	Notary / Travel Fee
		☐ Driver's license ☐ Credible Witness ☐ Passport ☐ Personally Known ☐ I D Card ☐ Other_____ ☐ I D. #_____		

Notary Public Record

23

Notarized Date/Time	Date of Document	Type of Documents	Service	Name, Phone #, address of signer	E-mail:
			☐ Acknowledgment ☐ Oath/Affirmation ☐ Jurat ☐ Other ————		Signature

Name, Phone #, address of witness	Signature of witness	Identity	Right Thumbprint	Notary / Travel Fee
		☐ Driver's license ☐ Credible Witness ☐ Passport ☐ Personally Known ☐ I D Card ☐ Other_____ ☐ I D. #_____		

Notary Public Record

24

Notarized Date/Time	Date of Document	Type of Documents	Service	Name, Phone #, address of signer	E-mail:
			☐ Acknowledgment ☐ Oath/Affirmation ☐ Jurat ☐ Other ————		Signature

Name, Phone #, address of witness	Signature of witness	Identity	Right Thumbprint	Notary / Travel Fee
		☐ Driver's license ☐ Credible Witness ☐ Passport ☐ Personally Known ☐ I D Card ☐ Other_____ ☐ I D. #_____		

25 Notary Public Record

Notarized Date/Time	Date of Document	Type of Documents	Service	Name, Phone #, address of signer	E-mail:
		_____	☐ Acknowledgment ☐ Oath/Affirmation ☐ Jurat ☐ Other _____	_____	Signature
_____	_____	_____		_____	

Name, Phone #, address of witness	Signature of witness	Identity	Right Thumbprint	Notary / Travel Fee
		☐ Driver's license ☐ Credible Witness ☐ Passport ☐ Personally Known ☐ I D Card ☐ Other_____ ☐ I D. # _____		

26 Notary Public Record

Notarized Date/Time	Date of Document	Type of Documents	Service	Name, Phone #, address of signer	E-mail:
		_____	☐ Acknowledgment ☐ Oath/Affirmation ☐ Jurat ☐ Other _____	_____	Signature
_____	_____	_____		_____	

Name, Phone #, address of witness	Signature of witness	Identity	Right Thumbprint	Notary / Travel Fee
		☐ Driver's license ☐ Credible Witness ☐ Passport ☐ Personally Known ☐ I D Card ☐ Other_____ ☐ I D. # _____		

27 Notary Public Record

Notarized Date/Time	Date of Document	Type of Documents	Service	Name, Phone #, address of signer	E-mail:
		_____	☐ Acknowledgment ☐ Oath/Affirmation ☐ Jurat ☐ Other _____	_____	Signature
_____	_____	_____		_____	

Name, Phone #, address of witness	Signature of witness	Identity	Right Thumbprint	Notary / Travel Fee
		☐ Driver's license ☐ Credible Witness ☐ Passport ☐ Personally Known ☐ I D Card ☐ Other_____ ☐ I D. # _____		

28 Notary Public Record

Notarized Date/Time	Date of Document	Type of Documents	Service	Name, Phone #, address of signer	E-mail:
_____ _____	_____	_____	☐ Acknowledgment ☐ Oath/Affirmation ☐ Jurat ☐ Other _____	_____ _____	Signature _____

Name, Phone #, address of witness	Signature of witness	Identity	Right Thumbprint	Notary / Travel Fee
_____ _____		☐ Driver's license ☐ Credible Witness ☐ Passport ☐ Personally Known ☐ I D Card ☐ Other_____ ☐ I D. # _____		

29 Notary Public Record

Notarized Date/Time	Date of Document	Type of Documents	Service	Name, Phone #, address of signer	E-mail:
_____ _____	_____	_____	☐ Acknowledgment ☐ Oath/Affirmation ☐ Jurat ☐ Other _____	_____ _____	Signature _____

Name, Phone #, address of witness	Signature of witness	Identity	Right Thumbprint	Notary / Travel Fee
_____ _____		☐ Driver's license ☐ Credible Witness ☐ Passport ☐ Personally Known ☐ I D Card ☐ Other_____ ☐ I D. # _____		

30 Notary Public Record

Notarized Date/Time	Date of Document	Type of Documents	Service	Name, Phone #, address of signer	E-mail:
_____ _____	_____	_____	☐ Acknowledgment ☐ Oath/Affirmation ☐ Jurat ☐ Other _____	_____ _____	Signature _____

Name, Phone #, address of witness	Signature of witness	Identity	Right Thumbprint	Notary / Travel Fee
_____ _____		☐ Driver's license ☐ Credible Witness ☐ Passport ☐ Personally Known ☐ I D Card ☐ Other_____ ☐ I D. # _____		

31 Notary Public Record

Notarized Date/Time	Date of Document	Type of Documents	Service	Name, Phone #, address of signer	E-mail:
		_____	☐ Acknowledgment ☐ Oath/Affirmation ☐ Jurat ☐ Other _____	_____	Signature
_____	_____	_____		_____	_____

Name, Phone #, address of witness	Signature of witness	Identity		Right Thumbprint	Notary / Travel Fee
_____		☐ Driver's license ☐ Credible Witness ☐ Passport ☐ Personally Known ☐ I D Card ☐ Other_____ ☐ I D. # _____			

32 Notary Public Record

Notarized Date/Time	Date of Document	Type of Documents	Service	Name, Phone #, address of signer	E-mail:
		_____	☐ Acknowledgment ☐ Oath/Affirmation ☐ Jurat ☐ Other _____	_____	Signature
_____	_____	_____		_____	_____

Name, Phone #, address of witness	Signature of witness	Identity		Right Thumbprint	Notary / Travel Fee
_____		☐ Driver's license ☐ Credible Witness ☐ Passport ☐ Personally Known ☐ I D Card ☐ Other_____ ☐ I D. # _____			

33 Notary Public Record

Notarized Date/Time	Date of Document	Type of Documents	Service	Name, Phone #, address of signer	E-mail:
		_____	☐ Acknowledgment ☐ Oath/Affirmation ☐ Jurat ☐ Other _____	_____	Signature
_____	_____	_____		_____	_____

Name, Phone #, address of witness	Signature of witness	Identity		Right Thumbprint	Notary / Travel Fee
_____		☐ Driver's license ☐ Credible Witness ☐ Passport ☐ Personally Known ☐ I D Card ☐ Other_____ ☐ I D. # _____			

34 Notary Public Record

Notarized Date/Time	Date of Document	Type of Documents	Service	Name, Phone #, address of signer	E-mail:
_____ _____	_____	_____ _____	☐ Acknowledgment ☐ Oath/Affirmation ☐ Jurat ☐ Other _____	_____ _____ _____	Signature _____

Name, Phone #, address of witness	Signature of witness	Identity		Right Thumbprint	Notary / Travel Fee
_____ _____		☐ Driver's license ☐ Credible Witness ☐ Passport ☐ Personally Known ☐ I D Card ☐ Other_____ ☐ I D. # _____			

35 Notary Public Record

Notarized Date/Time	Date of Document	Type of Documents	Service	Name, Phone #, address of signer	E-mail:
_____ _____	_____	_____ _____	☐ Acknowledgment ☐ Oath/Affirmation ☐ Jurat ☐ Other _____	_____ _____ _____	Signature _____

Name, Phone #, address of witness	Signature of witness	Identity		Right Thumbprint	Notary / Travel Fee
_____ _____		☐ Driver's license ☐ Credible Witness ☐ Passport ☐ Personally Known ☐ I D Card ☐ Other_____ ☐ I D. # _____			

36 Notary Public Record

Notarized Date/Time	Date of Document	Type of Documents	Service	Name, Phone #, address of signer	E-mail:
_____ _____	_____	_____ _____	☐ Acknowledgment ☐ Oath/Affirmation ☐ Jurat ☐ Other _____	_____ _____ _____	Signature _____

Name, Phone #, address of witness	Signature of witness	Identity		Right Thumbprint	Notary / Travel Fee
_____ _____		☐ Driver's license ☐ Credible Witness ☐ Passport ☐ Personally Known ☐ I D Card ☐ Other_____ ☐ I D. # _____			

37 Notary Public Record

Notarized Date/Time	Date of Document	Type of Documents	Service	Name, Phone #, address of signer	E-mail:
		_____	☐ Acknowledgment ☐ Oath/Affirmation ☐ Jurat ☐ Other _____	_____ _____	Signature _____

Name, Phone #, address of witness	Signature of witness	Identity	Right Thumbprint	Notary / Travel Fee
_____ _____		☐ Driver's license ☐ Credible Witness ☐ Passport ☐ Personally Known ☐ I D Card ☐ Other_____ ☐ I D. # _____		

38 Notary Public Record

Notarized Date/Time	Date of Document	Type of Documents	Service	Name, Phone #, address of signer	E-mail:
		_____	☐ Acknowledgment ☐ Oath/Affirmation ☐ Jurat ☐ Other _____	_____ _____	Signature _____

Name, Phone #, address of witness	Signature of witness	Identity	Right Thumbprint	Notary / Travel Fee
_____ _____		☐ Driver's license ☐ Credible Witness ☐ Passport ☐ Personally Known ☐ I D Card ☐ Other_____ ☐ I D. # _____		

39 Notary Public Record

Notarized Date/Time	Date of Document	Type of Documents	Service	Name, Phone #, address of signer	E-mail:
		_____	☐ Acknowledgment ☐ Oath/Affirmation ☐ Jurat ☐ Other _____	_____ _____	Signature _____

Name, Phone #, address of witness	Signature of witness	Identity	Right Thumbprint	Notary / Travel Fee
_____ _____		☐ Driver's license ☐ Credible Witness ☐ Passport ☐ Personally Known ☐ I D Card ☐ Other_____ ☐ I D. # _____		

40

Notary Public Record

Notarized Date/Time	Date of Document	Type of Documents	Service	Name, Phone #, address of signer	E-mail:
_____ _____	_____	_____ _____	☐ Acknowledgment ☐ Oath/Affirmation ☐ Jurat ☐ Other ————	_____ _____ _____	Signature _____

Name, Phone #, address of witness	Signature of witness	Identity		Right Thumbprint	Notary / Travel Fee
_____ _____	_____	☐ Driver's license ☐ Credible Witness ☐ Passport ☐ Personally Known ☐ I D Card ☐ Other_____ ☐ I D. #_____			

41

Notary Public Record

Notarized Date/Time	Date of Document	Type of Documents	Service	Name, Phone #, address of signer	E-mail:
_____ _____	_____	_____ _____	☐ Acknowledgment ☐ Oath/Affirmation ☐ Jurat ☐ Other ————	_____ _____ _____	Signature _____

Name, Phone #, address of witness	Signature of witness	Identity		Right Thumbprint	Notary / Travel Fee
_____ _____	_____	☐ Driver's license ☐ Credible Witness ☐ Passport ☐ Personally Known ☐ I D Card ☐ Other_____ ☐ I D. #_____			

42

Notary Public Record

Notarized Date/Time	Date of Document	Type of Documents	Service	Name, Phone #, address of signer	E-mail:
_____ _____	_____	_____ _____	☐ Acknowledgment ☐ Oath/Affirmation ☐ Jurat ☐ Other ————	_____ _____ _____	Signature _____

Name, Phone #, address of witness	Signature of witness	Identity		Right Thumbprint	Notary / Travel Fee
_____ _____	_____	☐ Driver's license ☐ Credible Witness ☐ Passport ☐ Personally Known ☐ I D Card ☐ Other_____ ☐ I D. #_____			

43 Notary Public Record

Notarized Date/Time	Date of Document	Type of Documents	Service	Name, Phone #, address of signer	E-mail:
			☐ Acknowledgment ☐ Oath/Affirmation ☐ Jurat ☐ Other _____		Signature

Name, Phone #, address of witness	Signature of witness	Identity	Right Thumbprint	Notary / Travel Fee
		☐ Driver's license ☐ Credible Witness ☐ Passport ☐ Personally Known ☐ I D Card ☐ Other_____ ☐ I D. # _____		

44 Notary Public Record

Notarized Date/Time	Date of Document	Type of Documents	Service	Name, Phone #, address of signer	E-mail:
			☐ Acknowledgment ☐ Oath/Affirmation ☐ Jurat ☐ Other _____		Signature

Name, Phone #, address of witness	Signature of witness	Identity	Right Thumbprint	Notary / Travel Fee
		☐ Driver's license ☐ Credible Witness ☐ Passport ☐ Personally Known ☐ I D Card ☐ Other_____ ☐ I D. # _____		

45 Notary Public Record

Notarized Date/Time	Date of Document	Type of Documents	Service	Name, Phone #, address of signer	E-mail:
			☐ Acknowledgment ☐ Oath/Affirmation ☐ Jurat ☐ Other _____		Signature

Name, Phone #, address of witness	Signature of witness	Identity	Right Thumbprint	Notary / Travel Fee
		☐ Driver's license ☐ Credible Witness ☐ Passport ☐ Personally Known ☐ I D Card ☐ Other_____ ☐ I D. # _____		

46 Notary Public Record

Notarized Date/Time	Date of Document	Type of Documents	Service	Name, Phone #, address of signer	E-mail:
		_____	☐ Acknowledgment ☐ Oath/Affirmation ☐ Jurat ☐ Other _____	_____	Signature
_____	_____	_____		_____	_____

Name, Phone #, address of witness	Signature of witness	Identity		Right Thumbprint	Notary / Travel Fee
_____		☐ Driver's license ☐ Credible Witness ☐ Passport ☐ Personally Known ☐ I D Card ☐ Other_____			
_____		☐ I D. # _____			

47 Notary Public Record

Notarized Date/Time	Date of Document	Type of Documents	Service	Name, Phone #, address of signer	E-mail:
		_____	☐ Acknowledgment ☐ Oath/Affirmation ☐ Jurat ☐ Other _____	_____	Signature
_____	_____	_____		_____	_____

Name, Phone #, address of witness	Signature of witness	Identity		Right Thumbprint	Notary / Travel Fee
_____		☐ Driver's license ☐ Credible Witness ☐ Passport ☐ Personally Known ☐ I D Card ☐ Other_____			
_____		☐ I D. # _____			

48 Notary Public Record

Notarized Date/Time	Date of Document	Type of Documents	Service	Name, Phone #, address of signer	E-mail:
		_____	☐ Acknowledgment ☐ Oath/Affirmation ☐ Jurat ☐ Other _____	_____	Signature
_____	_____	_____		_____	_____

Name, Phone #, address of witness	Signature of witness	Identity		Right Thumbprint	Notary / Travel Fee
_____		☐ Driver's license ☐ Credible Witness ☐ Passport ☐ Personally Known ☐ I D Card ☐ Other_____			
_____		☐ I D. # _____			

49 Notary Public Record

Notarized Date/Time	Date of Document	Type of Documents	Service	Name, Phone #, address of signer	E-mail:
		_____	☐ Acknowledgment ☐ Oath/Affirmation ☐ Jurat ☐ Other _____	_____	Signature
_____	_____	_____		_____	_____

Name, Phone #, address of witness	Signature of witness	Identity	Right Thumbprint	Notary / Travel Fee
_____		☐ Driver's license ☐ Credible Witness ☐ Passport ☐ Personally Known ☐ I D Card ☐ Other_____ ☐ I D. # _____		

50 Notary Public Record

Notarized Date/Time	Date of Document	Type of Documents	Service	Name, Phone #, address of signer	E-mail:
		_____	☐ Acknowledgment ☐ Oath/Affirmation ☐ Jurat ☐ Other _____	_____	Signature
_____	_____	_____		_____	_____

Name, Phone #, address of witness	Signature of witness	Identity	Right Thumbprint	Notary / Travel Fee
_____		☐ Driver's license ☐ Credible Witness ☐ Passport ☐ Personally Known ☐ I D Card ☐ Other_____ ☐ I D. # _____		

51 Notary Public Record

Notarized Date/Time	Date of Document	Type of Documents	Service	Name, Phone #, address of signer	E-mail:
		_____	☐ Acknowledgment ☐ Oath/Affirmation ☐ Jurat ☐ Other _____	_____	Signature
_____	_____	_____		_____	_____

Name, Phone #, address of witness	Signature of witness	Identity	Right Thumbprint	Notary / Travel Fee
_____		☐ Driver's license ☐ Credible Witness ☐ Passport ☐ Personally Known ☐ I D Card ☐ Other_____ ☐ I D. # _____		

52   *Notary Public Record*

Notarized Date/Time	Date of Document	Type of Documents	Service	Name, Phone #, address of signer	E-mail:
			☐ Acknowledgment ☐ Oath/Affirmation ☐ Jurat ☐ Other _____		Signature

Name, Phone #, address of witness	Signature of witness	Identity	Right Thumbprint	Notary / Travel Fee
		☐ Driver's license ☐ Credible Witness ☐ Passport ☐ Personally Known ☐ I D Card ☐ Other_____ ☐ I D. # _____		

53   *Notary Public Record*

Notarized Date/Time	Date of Document	Type of Documents	Service	Name, Phone #, address of signer	E-mail:
			☐ Acknowledgment ☐ Oath/Affirmation ☐ Jurat ☐ Other _____		Signature

Name, Phone #, address of witness	Signature of witness	Identity	Right Thumbprint	Notary / Travel Fee
		☐ Driver's license ☐ Credible Witness ☐ Passport ☐ Personally Known ☐ I D Card ☐ Other_____ ☐ I D. # _____		

54   *Notary Public Record*

Notarized Date/Time	Date of Document	Type of Documents	Service	Name, Phone #, address of signer	E-mail:
			☐ Acknowledgment ☐ Oath/Affirmation ☐ Jurat ☐ Other _____		Signature

Name, Phone #, address of witness	Signature of witness	Identity	Right Thumbprint	Notary / Travel Fee
		☐ Driver's license ☐ Credible Witness ☐ Passport ☐ Personally Known ☐ I D Card ☐ Other_____ ☐ I D. # _____		

55 Notary Public Record

Notarized Date/Time	Date of Document	Type of Documents	Service	Name, Phone #, address of signer	E-mail:
			☐ Acknowledgment ☐ Oath/Affirmation ☐ Jurat ☐ Other _____		Signature

Name, Phone #, address of witness	Signature of witness	Identity	Right Thumbprint	Notary / Travel Fee
		☐ Driver's license ☐ Credible Witness ☐ Passport ☐ Personally Known ☐ I D Card ☐ Other_____ ☐ I D. # _____		

56 Notary Public Record

Notarized Date/Time	Date of Document	Type of Documents	Service	Name, Phone #, address of signer	E-mail:
			☐ Acknowledgment ☐ Oath/Affirmation ☐ Jurat ☐ Other _____		Signature

Name, Phone #, address of witness	Signature of witness	Identity	Right Thumbprint	Notary / Travel Fee
		☐ Driver's license ☐ Credible Witness ☐ Passport ☐ Personally Known ☐ I D Card ☐ Other_____ ☐ I D. # _____		

57 Notary Public Record

Notarized Date/Time	Date of Document	Type of Documents	Service	Name, Phone #, address of signer	E-mail:
			☐ Acknowledgment ☐ Oath/Affirmation ☐ Jurat ☐ Other _____		Signature

Name, Phone #, address of witness	Signature of witness	Identity	Right Thumbprint	Notary / Travel Fee
		☐ Driver's license ☐ Credible Witness ☐ Passport ☐ Personally Known ☐ I D Card ☐ Other_____ ☐ I D. # _____		

58 Notary Public Record

Notarized Date/Time	Date of Document	Type of Documents	Service	Name, Phone #, address of signer	E-mail:
			☐ Acknowledgment ☐ Oath/Affirmation ☐ Jurat ☐ Other _____		Signature

Name, Phone #, address of witness	Signature of witness	Identity	Right Thumbprint	Notary / Travel Fee
		☐ Driver's license ☐ Credible Witness ☐ Passport ☐ Personally Known ☐ I D Card ☐ Other_____ ☐ I D. # _____		

59 Notary Public Record

Notarized Date/Time	Date of Document	Type of Documents	Service	Name, Phone #, address of signer	E-mail:
			☐ Acknowledgment ☐ Oath/Affirmation ☐ Jurat ☐ Other _____		Signature

Name, Phone #, address of witness	Signature of witness	Identity	Right Thumbprint	Notary / Travel Fee
		☐ Driver's license ☐ Credible Witness ☐ Passport ☐ Personally Known ☐ I D Card ☐ Other_____ ☐ I D. # _____		

60 Notary Public Record

Notarized Date/Time	Date of Document	Type of Documents	Service	Name, Phone #, address of signer	E-mail:
			☐ Acknowledgment ☐ Oath/Affirmation ☐ Jurat ☐ Other _____		Signature

Name, Phone #, address of witness	Signature of witness	Identity	Right Thumbprint	Notary / Travel Fee
		☐ Driver's license ☐ Credible Witness ☐ Passport ☐ Personally Known ☐ I D Card ☐ Other_____ ☐ I D. # _____		

61 Notary Public Record

Notarized Date/Time	Date of Document	Type of Documents	Service	Name, Phone #, address of signer	E-mail:
		_____	☐ Acknowledgment ☐ Oath/Affirmation ☐ Jurat ☐ Other ————	_____	Signature
_____	_____	_____		_____	
		_____		_____	_____

Name, Phone #, address of witness	Signature of witness	Identity	Right Thumbprint	Notary / Travel Fee
_____ _____ 		☐ Driver's license ☐ Credible Witness ☐ Passport ☐ Personally Known ☐ I D Card ☐ Other_____ ☐ I D. # _____		

62 Notary Public Record

Notarized Date/Time	Date of Document	Type of Documents	Service	Name, Phone #, address of signer	E-mail:
		_____	☐ Acknowledgment ☐ Oath/Affirmation ☐ Jurat ☐ Other ————	_____	Signature
_____	_____	_____		_____	
		_____		_____	_____

Name, Phone #, address of witness	Signature of witness	Identity	Right Thumbprint	Notary / Travel Fee
_____ _____ 		☐ Driver's license ☐ Credible Witness ☐ Passport ☐ Personally Known ☐ I D Card ☐ Other_____ ☐ I D. # _____		

63 Notary Public Record

Notarized Date/Time	Date of Document	Type of Documents	Service	Name, Phone #, address of signer	E-mail:
		_____	☐ Acknowledgment ☐ Oath/Affirmation ☐ Jurat ☐ Other ————	_____	Signature
_____	_____	_____		_____	
		_____		_____	_____

Name, Phone #, address of witness	Signature of witness	Identity	Right Thumbprint	Notary / Travel Fee
_____ _____ 		☐ Driver's license ☐ Credible Witness ☐ Passport ☐ Personally Known ☐ I D Card ☐ Other_____ ☐ I D. # _____		

64 Notary Public Record

Notarized Date/Time	Date of Document	Type of Documents	Service	Name, Phone #, address of signer	E-mail:
			☐ Acknowledgment ☐ Oath/Affirmation ☐ Jurat ☐ Other ————		Signature

Name, Phone #, address of witness	Signature of witness	Identity	Right Thumbprint	Notary / Travel Fee
		☐ Driver's license ☐ Credible Witness ☐ Passport ☐ Personally Known ☐ I D Card ☐ Other_____ ☐ I D. # _____		

65 Notary Public Record

Notarized Date/Time	Date of Document	Type of Documents	Service	Name, Phone #, address of signer	E-mail:
			☐ Acknowledgment ☐ Oath/Affirmation ☐ Jurat ☐ Other ————		Signature

Name, Phone #, address of witness	Signature of witness	Identity	Right Thumbprint	Notary / Travel Fee
		☐ Driver's license ☐ Credible Witness ☐ Passport ☐ Personally Known ☐ I D Card ☐ Other_____ ☐ I D. # _____		

66 Notary Public Record

Notarized Date/Time	Date of Document	Type of Documents	Service	Name, Phone #, address of signer	E-mail:
			☐ Acknowledgment ☐ Oath/Affirmation ☐ Jurat ☐ Other ————		Signature

Name, Phone #, address of witness	Signature of witness	Identity	Right Thumbprint	Notary / Travel Fee
		☐ Driver's license ☐ Credible Witness ☐ Passport ☐ Personally Known ☐ I D Card ☐ Other_____ ☐ I D. # _____		

67 Notary Public Record

Notarized Date/Time	Date of Document	Type of Documents	Service	Name, Phone #, address of signer	E-mail:
			☐ Acknowledgment ☐ Oath/Affirmation ☐ Jurat ☐ Other _____		Signature

Name, Phone #, address of witness	Signature of witness	Identity	Right Thumbprint	Notary / Travel Fee
		☐ Driver's license ☐ Credible Witness ☐ Passport ☐ Personally Known ☐ I D Card ☐ Other_____ ☐ I D. # _____		

68 Notary Public Record

Notarized Date/Time	Date of Document	Type of Documents	Service	Name, Phone #, address of signer	E-mail:
			☐ Acknowledgment ☐ Oath/Affirmation ☐ Jurat ☐ Other _____		Signature

Name, Phone #, address of witness	Signature of witness	Identity	Right Thumbprint	Notary / Travel Fee
		☐ Driver's license ☐ Credible Witness ☐ Passport ☐ Personally Known ☐ I D Card ☐ Other_____ ☐ I D. # _____		

69 Notary Public Record

Notarized Date/Time	Date of Document	Type of Documents	Service	Name, Phone #, address of signer	E-mail:
			☐ Acknowledgment ☐ Oath/Affirmation ☐ Jurat ☐ Other _____		Signature

Name, Phone #, address of witness	Signature of witness	Identity	Right Thumbprint	Notary / Travel Fee
		☐ Driver's license ☐ Credible Witness ☐ Passport ☐ Personally Known ☐ I D Card ☐ Other_____ ☐ I D. # _____		

70 Notary Public Record

Notarized Date/Time	Date of Document	Type of Documents	Service	Name, Phone #, address of signer	E-mail:
			☐ Acknowledgment ☐ Oath/Affirmation ☐ Jurat ☐ Other _____		Signature

Name, Phone #, address of witness	Signature of witness	Identity	Right Thumbprint	Notary / Travel Fee
		☐ Driver's license ☐ Credible Witness ☐ Passport ☐ Personally Known ☐ I D Card ☐ Other_____ ☐ I D. # _____		

71 Notary Public Record

Notarized Date/Time	Date of Document	Type of Documents	Service	Name, Phone #, address of signer	E-mail:
			☐ Acknowledgment ☐ Oath/Affirmation ☐ Jurat ☐ Other _____		Signature

Name, Phone #, address of witness	Signature of witness	Identity	Right Thumbprint	Notary / Travel Fee
		☐ Driver's license ☐ Credible Witness ☐ Passport ☐ Personally Known ☐ I D Card ☐ Other_____ ☐ I D. # _____		

72 Notary Public Record

Notarized Date/Time	Date of Document	Type of Documents	Service	Name, Phone #, address of signer	E-mail:
			☐ Acknowledgment ☐ Oath/Affirmation ☐ Jurat ☐ Other _____		Signature

Name, Phone #, address of witness	Signature of witness	Identity	Right Thumbprint	Notary / Travel Fee
		☐ Driver's license ☐ Credible Witness ☐ Passport ☐ Personally Known ☐ I D Card ☐ Other_____ ☐ I D. # _____		

73 Notary Public Record

Notarized Date/Time	Date of Document	Type of Documents	Service	Name, Phone #, address of signer	E-mail:
		_____	☐ Acknowledgment ☐ Oath/Affirmation ☐ Jurat ☐ Other _____	_____	Signature
_____	_____	_____		_____	
_____		_____		_____	_____

Name, Phone #, address of witness	Signature of witness	Identity	Right Thumbprint	Notary / Travel Fee
_____		☐ Driver's license ☐ Credible Witness ☐ Passport ☐ Personally Known ☐ I D Card ☐ Other_____		
_____		☐ I D. # _____		

74 Notary Public Record

Notarized Date/Time	Date of Document	Type of Documents	Service	Name, Phone #, address of signer	E-mail:
		_____	☐ Acknowledgment ☐ Oath/Affirmation ☐ Jurat ☐ Other _____	_____	Signature
_____	_____	_____		_____	
_____		_____		_____	_____

Name, Phone #, address of witness	Signature of witness	Identity	Right Thumbprint	Notary / Travel Fee
_____		☐ Driver's license ☐ Credible Witness ☐ Passport ☐ Personally Known ☐ I D Card ☐ Other_____		
_____		☐ I D. # _____		

75 Notary Public Record

Notarized Date/Time	Date of Document	Type of Documents	Service	Name, Phone #, address of signer	E-mail:
		_____	☐ Acknowledgment ☐ Oath/Affirmation ☐ Jurat ☐ Other _____	_____	Signature
_____	_____	_____		_____	
_____		_____		_____	_____

Name, Phone #, address of witness	Signature of witness	Identity	Right Thumbprint	Notary / Travel Fee
_____		☐ Driver's license ☐ Credible Witness ☐ Passport ☐ Personally Known ☐ I D Card ☐ Other_____		
_____		☐ I D. # _____		

76 Notary Public Record

Notarized Date/Time	Date of Document	Type of Documents	Service	Name, Phone #, address of signer	E-mail:
			☐ Acknowledgment ☐ Oath/Affirmation ☐ Jurat ☐ Other ————		Signature

Name, Phone #, address of witness	Signature of witness	Identity	Right Thumbprint	Notary / Travel Fee
		☐ Driver's license ☐ Credible Witness ☐ Passport ☐ Personally Known ☐ I D Card ☐ Other_____ ☐ I D. # _____		

77 Notary Public Record

Notarized Date/Time	Date of Document	Type of Documents	Service	Name, Phone #, address of signer	E-mail:
			☐ Acknowledgment ☐ Oath/Affirmation ☐ Jurat ☐ Other ————		Signature

Name, Phone #, address of witness	Signature of witness	Identity	Right Thumbprint	Notary / Travel Fee
		☐ Driver's license ☐ Credible Witness ☐ Passport ☐ Personally Known ☐ I D Card ☐ Other_____ ☐ I D. # _____		

78 Notary Public Record

Notarized Date/Time	Date of Document	Type of Documents	Service	Name, Phone #, address of signer	E-mail:
			☐ Acknowledgment ☐ Oath/Affirmation ☐ Jurat ☐ Other ————		Signature

Name, Phone #, address of witness	Signature of witness	Identity	Right Thumbprint	Notary / Travel Fee
		☐ Driver's license ☐ Credible Witness ☐ Passport ☐ Personally Known ☐ I D Card ☐ Other_____ ☐ I D. # _____		

79 Notary Public Record

Notarized Date/Time	Date of Document	Type of Documents	Service	Name, Phone #, address of signer	E-mail:
		_____	☐ Acknowledgment ☐ Oath/Affirmation ☐ Jurat ☐ Other _____	_____	Signature
_____	_____	_____		_____	
_____		_____		_____	_____

Name, Phone #, address of witness	Signature of witness	Identity	Right Thumbprint	Notary / Travel Fee
_____ _____		☐ Driver's license ☐ Credible Witness ☐ Passport ☐ Personally Known ☐ I D Card ☐ Other_____ ☐ I D. # _____		

80 Notary Public Record

Notarized Date/Time	Date of Document	Type of Documents	Service	Name, Phone #, address of signer	E-mail:
		_____	☐ Acknowledgment ☐ Oath/Affirmation ☐ Jurat ☐ Other _____	_____	Signature
_____	_____	_____		_____	
_____		_____		_____	_____

Name, Phone #, address of witness	Signature of witness	Identity	Right Thumbprint	Notary / Travel Fee
_____ _____		☐ Driver's license ☐ Credible Witness ☐ Passport ☐ Personally Known ☐ I D Card ☐ Other_____ ☐ I D. # _____		

81 Notary Public Record

Notarized Date/Time	Date of Document	Type of Documents	Service	Name, Phone #, address of signer	E-mail:
		_____	☐ Acknowledgment ☐ Oath/Affirmation ☐ Jurat ☐ Other _____	_____	Signature
_____	_____	_____		_____	
_____		_____		_____	_____

Name, Phone #, address of witness	Signature of witness	Identity	Right Thumbprint	Notary / Travel Fee
_____ _____		☐ Driver's license ☐ Credible Witness ☐ Passport ☐ Personally Known ☐ I D Card ☐ Other_____ ☐ I D. # _____		

82 Notary Public Record

Notarized Date/Time	Date of Document	Type of Documents	Service	Name, Phone #, address of signer	E-mail:
			☐ Acknowledgment ☐ Oath/Affirmation ☐ Jurat ☐ Other _____		Signature

Name, Phone #, address of witness	Signature of witness	Identity	Right Thumbprint	Notary / Travel Fee
		☐ Driver's license ☐ Credible Witness ☐ Passport ☐ Personally Known ☐ I D Card ☐ Other_____ ☐ I D. # _____		

83 Notary Public Record

Notarized Date/Time	Date of Document	Type of Documents	Service	Name, Phone #, address of signer	E-mail:
			☐ Acknowledgment ☐ Oath/Affirmation ☐ Jurat ☐ Other _____		Signature

Name, Phone #, address of witness	Signature of witness	Identity	Right Thumbprint	Notary / Travel Fee
		☐ Driver's license ☐ Credible Witness ☐ Passport ☐ Personally Known ☐ I D Card ☐ Other_____ ☐ I D. # _____		

84 Notary Public Record

Notarized Date/Time	Date of Document	Type of Documents	Service	Name, Phone #, address of signer	E-mail:
			☐ Acknowledgment ☐ Oath/Affirmation ☐ Jurat ☐ Other _____		Signature

Name, Phone #, address of witness	Signature of witness	Identity	Right Thumbprint	Notary / Travel Fee
		☐ Driver's license ☐ Credible Witness ☐ Passport ☐ Personally Known ☐ I D Card ☐ Other_____ ☐ I D. # _____		

85   *Notary Public Record*

Notarized Date/Time	Date of Document	Type of Documents	Service	Name, Phone #, address of signer	E-mail:
			☐ Acknowledgment ☐ Oath/Affirmation ☐ Jurat ☐ Other _____		Signature

Name, Phone #, address of witness	Signature of witness	Identity	Right Thumbprint	Notary / Travel Fee
		☐ Driver's license ☐ Credible Witness ☐ Passport ☐ Personally Known ☐ I D Card ☐ Other_____ ☐ I D. # _____		

---

86   *Notary Public Record*

Notarized Date/Time	Date of Document	Type of Documents	Service	Name, Phone #, address of signer	E-mail:
			☐ Acknowledgment ☐ Oath/Affirmation ☐ Jurat ☐ Other _____		Signature

Name, Phone #, address of witness	Signature of witness	Identity	Right Thumbprint	Notary / Travel Fee
		☐ Driver's license ☐ Credible Witness ☐ Passport ☐ Personally Known ☐ I D Card ☐ Other_____ ☐ I D. # _____		

---

87   *Notary Public Record*

Notarized Date/Time	Date of Document	Type of Documents	Service	Name, Phone #, address of signer	E-mail:
			☐ Acknowledgment ☐ Oath/Affirmation ☐ Jurat ☐ Other _____		Signature

Name, Phone #, address of witness	Signature of witness	Identity	Right Thumbprint	Notary / Travel Fee
		☐ Driver's license ☐ Credible Witness ☐ Passport ☐ Personally Known ☐ I D Card ☐ Other_____ ☐ I D. # _____		

88   Notary Public Record

Notarized Date/Time	Date of Document	Type of Documents	Service	Name, Phone #, address of signer	E-mail:
			☐ Acknowledgment ☐ Oath/Affirmation ☐ Jurat ☐ Other ————		Signature

Name, Phone #, address of witness	Signature of witness	Identity	Right Thumbprint	Notary / Travel Fee
		☐ Driver's license ☐ Credible Witness ☐ Passport ☐ Personally Known ☐ I D Card ☐ Other_____ ☐ I D. # _____		

89   Notary Public Record

Notarized Date/Time	Date of Document	Type of Documents	Service	Name, Phone #, address of signer	E-mail:
			☐ Acknowledgment ☐ Oath/Affirmation ☐ Jurat ☐ Other ————		Signature

Name, Phone #, address of witness	Signature of witness	Identity	Right Thumbprint	Notary / Travel Fee
		☐ Driver's license ☐ Credible Witness ☐ Passport ☐ Personally Known ☐ I D Card ☐ Other_____ ☐ I D. # _____		

90   Notary Public Record

Notarized Date/Time	Date of Document	Type of Documents	Service	Name, Phone #, address of signer	E-mail:
			☐ Acknowledgment ☐ Oath/Affirmation ☐ Jurat ☐ Other ————		Signature

Name, Phone #, address of witness	Signature of witness	Identity	Right Thumbprint	Notary / Travel Fee
		☐ Driver's license ☐ Credible Witness ☐ Passport ☐ Personally Known ☐ I D Card ☐ Other_____ ☐ I D. # _____		

91 Notary Public Record

Notarized Date/Time	Date of Document	Type of Documents	Service	Name, Phone #, address of signer	E-mail:
			☐ Acknowledgment ☐ Oath/Affirmation ☐ Jurat ☐ Other ————		Signature

Name, Phone #, address of witness	Signature of witness	Identity	Right Thumbprint	Notary / Travel Fee
		☐ Driver's license ☐ Credible Witness ☐ Passport ☐ Personally Known ☐ I D Card ☐ Other_____ ☐ I D. # _____		

92 Notary Public Record

Notarized Date/Time	Date of Document	Type of Documents	Service	Name, Phone #, address of signer	E-mail:
			☐ Acknowledgment ☐ Oath/Affirmation ☐ Jurat ☐ Other ————		Signature

Name, Phone #, address of witness	Signature of witness	Identity	Right Thumbprint	Notary / Travel Fee
		☐ Driver's license ☐ Credible Witness ☐ Passport ☐ Personally Known ☐ I D Card ☐ Other_____ ☐ I D. # _____		

93 Notary Public Record

Notarized Date/Time	Date of Document	Type of Documents	Service	Name, Phone #, address of signer	E-mail:
			☐ Acknowledgment ☐ Oath/Affirmation ☐ Jurat ☐ Other ————		Signature

Name, Phone #, address of witness	Signature of witness	Identity	Right Thumbprint	Notary / Travel Fee
		☐ Driver's license ☐ Credible Witness ☐ Passport ☐ Personally Known ☐ I D Card ☐ Other_____ ☐ I D. # _____		

Notary Public Record

94

Notarized Date/Time	Date of Document	Type of Documents	Service	Name, Phone #, address of signer	E-mail:
			☐ Acknowledgment ☐ Oath/Affirmation ☐ Jurat ☐ Other _____		Signature

Name, Phone #, address of witness	Signature of witness	Identity	Right Thumbprint	Notary / Travel Fee
		☐ Driver's license ☐ Credible Witness ☐ Passport ☐ Personally Known ☐ I D Card ☐ Other _____ ☐ I D. # _____		

Notary Public Record

95

Notarized Date/Time	Date of Document	Type of Documents	Service	Name, Phone #, address of signer	E-mail:
			☐ Acknowledgment ☐ Oath/Affirmation ☐ Jurat ☐ Other _____		Signature

Name, Phone #, address of witness	Signature of witness	Identity	Right Thumbprint	Notary / Travel Fee
		☐ Driver's license ☐ Credible Witness ☐ Passport ☐ Personally Known ☐ I D Card ☐ Other _____ ☐ I D. # _____		

Notary Public Record

96

Notarized Date/Time	Date of Document	Type of Documents	Service	Name, Phone #, address of signer	E-mail:
			☐ Acknowledgment ☐ Oath/Affirmation ☐ Jurat ☐ Other _____		Signature

Name, Phone #, address of witness	Signature of witness	Identity	Right Thumbprint	Notary / Travel Fee
		☐ Driver's license ☐ Credible Witness ☐ Passport ☐ Personally Known ☐ I D Card ☐ Other _____ ☐ I D. # _____		

Notary Public Record

97

Notarized Date/Time	Date of Document	Type of Documents	Service	Name, Phone #, address of signer	E-mail:
			☐ Acknowledgment ☐ Oath/Affirmation ☐ Jurat ☐ Other _____		Signature

Name, Phone #, address of witness	Signature of witness	Identity	Right Thumbprint	Notary / Travel Fee
		☐ Driver's license ☐ Credible Witness ☐ Passport ☐ Personally Known ☐ I D Card ☐ Other_____ ☐ I D. # _____		

Notary Public Record

98

Notarized Date/Time	Date of Document	Type of Documents	Service	Name, Phone #, address of signer	E-mail:
			☐ Acknowledgment ☐ Oath/Affirmation ☐ Jurat ☐ Other _____		Signature

Name, Phone #, address of witness	Signature of witness	Identity	Right Thumbprint	Notary / Travel Fee
		☐ Driver's license ☐ Credible Witness ☐ Passport ☐ Personally Known ☐ I D Card ☐ Other_____ ☐ I D. # _____		

Notary Public Record

99

Notarized Date/Time	Date of Document	Type of Documents	Service	Name, Phone #, address of signer	E-mail:
			☐ Acknowledgment ☐ Oath/Affirmation ☐ Jurat ☐ Other _____		Signature

Name, Phone #, address of witness	Signature of witness	Identity	Right Thumbprint	Notary / Travel Fee
		☐ Driver's license ☐ Credible Witness ☐ Passport ☐ Personally Known ☐ I D Card ☐ Other_____ ☐ I D. # _____		

100 Notary Public Record

Notarized Date/Time	Date of Document	Type of Documents	Service	Name, Phone #, address of signer	E-mail:
			☐ Acknowledgment ☐ Oath/Affirmation ☐ Jurat ☐ Other _____		Signature

Name, Phone #, address of witness	Signature of witness	Identity		Right Thumbprint	Notary / Travel Fee
		☐ Driver's license ☐ Credible Witness ☐ Passport ☐ Personally Known ☐ I D Card ☐ Other_____ ☐ I D. # _____			

101 Notary Public Record

Notarized Date/Time	Date of Document	Type of Documents	Service	Name, Phone #, address of signer	E-mail:
			☐ Acknowledgment ☐ Oath/Affirmation ☐ Jurat ☐ Other _____		Signature

Name, Phone #, address of witness	Signature of witness	Identity		Right Thumbprint	Notary / Travel Fee
		☐ Driver's license ☐ Credible Witness ☐ Passport ☐ Personally Known ☐ I D Card ☐ Other_____ ☐ I D. # _____			

102 Notary Public Record

Notarized Date/Time	Date of Document	Type of Documents	Service	Name, Phone #, address of signer	E-mail:
			☐ Acknowledgment ☐ Oath/Affirmation ☐ Jurat ☐ Other _____		Signature

Name, Phone #, address of witness	Signature of witness	Identity		Right Thumbprint	Notary / Travel Fee
		☐ Driver's license ☐ Credible Witness ☐ Passport ☐ Personally Known ☐ I D Card ☐ Other_____ ☐ I D. # _____			

103 Notary Public Record

Notarized Date/Time	Date of Document	Type of Documents	Service	Name, Phone #, address of signer	E-mail:
			☐ Acknowledgment ☐ Oath/Affirmation ☐ Jurat ☐ Other _____		Signature

Name, Phone #, address of witness	Signature of witness	Identity	Right Thumbprint	Notary / Travel Fee
		☐ Driver's license ☐ Credible Witness ☐ Passport ☐ Personally Known ☐ I D Card ☐ Other_____ ☐ I D. # _____		

104 Notary Public Record

Notarized Date/Time	Date of Document	Type of Documents	Service	Name, Phone #, address of signer	E-mail:
			☐ Acknowledgment ☐ Oath/Affirmation ☐ Jurat ☐ Other _____		Signature

Name, Phone #, address of witness	Signature of witness	Identity	Right Thumbprint	Notary / Travel Fee
		☐ Driver's license ☐ Credible Witness ☐ Passport ☐ Personally Known ☐ I D Card ☐ Other_____ ☐ I D. # _____		

105 Notary Public Record

Notarized Date/Time	Date of Document	Type of Documents	Service	Name, Phone #, address of signer	E-mail:
			☐ Acknowledgment ☐ Oath/Affirmation ☐ Jurat ☐ Other _____		Signature

Name, Phone #, address of witness	Signature of witness	Identity	Right Thumbprint	Notary / Travel Fee
		☐ Driver's license ☐ Credible Witness ☐ Passport ☐ Personally Known ☐ I D Card ☐ Other_____ ☐ I D. # _____		

106 — Notary Public Record

Notarized Date/Time	Date of Document	Type of Documents	Service	Name, Phone #, address of signer	E-mail:
			☐ Acknowledgment ☐ Oath/Affirmation ☐ Jurat ☐ Other _____		Signature

Name, Phone #, address of witness	Signature of witness	Identity	Right Thumbprint	Notary / Travel Fee
		☐ Driver's license ☐ Credible Witness ☐ Passport ☐ Personally Known ☐ I D Card ☐ Other _____ ☐ I D. # _____		

107 — Notary Public Record

Notarized Date/Time	Date of Document	Type of Documents	Service	Name, Phone #, address of signer	E-mail:
			☐ Acknowledgment ☐ Oath/Affirmation ☐ Jurat ☐ Other _____		Signature

Name, Phone #, address of witness	Signature of witness	Identity	Right Thumbprint	Notary / Travel Fee
		☐ Driver's license ☐ Credible Witness ☐ Passport ☐ Personally Known ☐ I D Card ☐ Other _____ ☐ I D. # _____		

108 — Notary Public Record

Notarized Date/Time	Date of Document	Type of Documents	Service	Name, Phone #, address of signer	E-mail:
			☐ Acknowledgment ☐ Oath/Affirmation ☐ Jurat ☐ Other _____		Signature

Name, Phone #, address of witness	Signature of witness	Identity	Right Thumbprint	Notary / Travel Fee
		☐ Driver's license ☐ Credible Witness ☐ Passport ☐ Personally Known ☐ I D Card ☐ Other _____ ☐ I D. # _____		

109 Notary Public Record

Notarized Date/Time	Date of Document	Type of Documents	Service	Name, Phone #, address of signer	E-mail:
		_____	☐ Acknowledgment ☐ Oath/Affirmation ☐ Jurat ☐ Other _____	_____	Signature
_____	_____	_____		_____	_____

Name, Phone #, address of witness	Signature of witness	Identity	Right Thumbprint	Notary / Travel Fee
_____		☐ Driver's license ☐ Credible Witness ☐ Passport ☐ Personally Known ☐ I D Card ☐ Other_____ ☐ I D. # _____		

110 Notary Public Record

Notarized Date/Time	Date of Document	Type of Documents	Service	Name, Phone #, address of signer	E-mail:
		_____	☐ Acknowledgment ☐ Oath/Affirmation ☐ Jurat ☐ Other _____	_____	Signature
_____	_____	_____		_____	_____

Name, Phone #, address of witness	Signature of witness	Identity	Right Thumbprint	Notary / Travel Fee
_____		☐ Driver's license ☐ Credible Witness ☐ Passport ☐ Personally Known ☐ I D Card ☐ Other_____ ☐ I D. # _____		

111 Notary Public Record

Notarized Date/Time	Date of Document	Type of Documents	Service	Name, Phone #, address of signer	E-mail:
		_____	☐ Acknowledgment ☐ Oath/Affirmation ☐ Jurat ☐ Other _____	_____	Signature
_____	_____	_____		_____	_____

Name, Phone #, address of witness	Signature of witness	Identity	Right Thumbprint	Notary / Travel Fee
_____		☐ Driver's license ☐ Credible Witness ☐ Passport ☐ Personally Known ☐ I D Card ☐ Other_____ ☐ I D. # _____		

112   *Notary Public Record*

Notarized Date/Time	Date of Document	Type of Documents	Service	Name, Phone #, address of signer	E-mail:
			☐ Acknowledgment ☐ Oath/Affirmation ☐ Jurat ☐ Other ———		Signature

Name, Phone #, address of witness	Signature of witness	Identity	Right Thumbprint	Notary / Travel Fee
		☐ Driver's license ☐ Credible Witness ☐ Passport ☐ Personally Known ☐ I D Card ☐ Other_____ ☐ I D. # _____		

113   *Notary Public Record*

Notarized Date/Time	Date of Document	Type of Documents	Service	Name, Phone #, address of signer	E-mail:
			☐ Acknowledgment ☐ Oath/Affirmation ☐ Jurat ☐ Other ———		Signature

Name, Phone #, address of witness	Signature of witness	Identity	Right Thumbprint	Notary / Travel Fee
		☐ Driver's license ☐ Credible Witness ☐ Passport ☐ Personally Known ☐ I D Card ☐ Other_____ ☐ I D. # _____		

114   *Notary Public Record*

Notarized Date/Time	Date of Document	Type of Documents	Service	Name, Phone #, address of signer	E-mail:
			☐ Acknowledgment ☐ Oath/Affirmation ☐ Jurat ☐ Other ———		Signature

Name, Phone #, address of witness	Signature of witness	Identity	Right Thumbprint	Notary / Travel Fee
		☐ Driver's license ☐ Credible Witness ☐ Passport ☐ Personally Known ☐ I D Card ☐ Other_____ ☐ I D. # _____		

Notary Public Record

115

Notarized Date/Time	Date of Document	Type of Documents	Service	Name, Phone #, address of signer	E-mail:
			☐ Acknowledgment ☐ Oath/Affirmation ☐ Jurat ☐ Other _____		Signature

Name, Phone #, address of witness	Signature of witness	Identity	Right Thumbprint	Notary / Travel Fee
		☐ Driver's license ☐ Credible Witness ☐ Passport ☐ Personally Known ☐ I D Card ☐ Other_____ ☐ I D. # _____		

Notary Public Record

116

Notarized Date/Time	Date of Document	Type of Documents	Service	Name, Phone #, address of signer	E-mail:
			☐ Acknowledgment ☐ Oath/Affirmation ☐ Jurat ☐ Other _____		Signature

Name, Phone #, address of witness	Signature of witness	Identity	Right Thumbprint	Notary / Travel Fee
		☐ Driver's license ☐ Credible Witness ☐ Passport ☐ Personally Known ☐ I D Card ☐ Other_____ ☐ I D. # _____		

Notary Public Record

117

Notarized Date/Time	Date of Document	Type of Documents	Service	Name, Phone #, address of signer	E-mail:
			☐ Acknowledgment ☐ Oath/Affirmation ☐ Jurat ☐ Other _____		Signature

Name, Phone #, address of witness	Signature of witness	Identity	Right Thumbprint	Notary / Travel Fee
		☐ Driver's license ☐ Credible Witness ☐ Passport ☐ Personally Known ☐ I D Card ☐ Other_____ ☐ I D. # _____		

118 Notary Public Record

Notarized Date/Time	Date of Document	Type of Documents	Service	Name, Phone #, address of signer	E-mail:
			☐ Acknowledgment ☐ Oath/Affirmation ☐ Jurat ☐ Other _____		Signature

Name, Phone #, address of witness	Signature of witness	Identity	Right Thumbprint	Notary / Travel Fee
		☐ Driver's license ☐ Credible Witness ☐ Passport ☐ Personally Known ☐ I D Card ☐ Other_____ ☐ I D. # _____		

119 Notary Public Record

Notarized Date/Time	Date of Document	Type of Documents	Service	Name, Phone #, address of signer	E-mail:
			☐ Acknowledgment ☐ Oath/Affirmation ☐ Jurat ☐ Other _____		Signature

Name, Phone #, address of witness	Signature of witness	Identity	Right Thumbprint	Notary / Travel Fee
		☐ Driver's license ☐ Credible Witness ☐ Passport ☐ Personally Known ☐ I D Card ☐ Other_____ ☐ I D. # _____		

120 Notary Public Record

Notarized Date/Time	Date of Document	Type of Documents	Service	Name, Phone #, address of signer	E-mail:
			☐ Acknowledgment ☐ Oath/Affirmation ☐ Jurat ☐ Other _____		Signature

Name, Phone #, address of witness	Signature of witness	Identity	Right Thumbprint	Notary / Travel Fee
		☐ Driver's license ☐ Credible Witness ☐ Passport ☐ Personally Known ☐ I D Card ☐ Other_____ ☐ I D. # _____		

121 Notary Public Record

Notarized Date/Time	Date of Document	Type of Documents	Service	Name, Phone #, address of signer	E-mail:
			☐ Acknowledgment ☐ Oath/Affirmation ☐ Jurat ☐ Other _____		Signature

Name, Phone #, address of witness	Signature of witness	Identity	Right Thumbprint	Notary / Travel Fee
		☐ Driver's license ☐ Credible Witness ☐ Passport ☐ Personally Known ☐ I D Card ☐ Other_____ ☐ I D. # _____		

122 Notary Public Record

Notarized Date/Time	Date of Document	Type of Documents	Service	Name, Phone #, address of signer	E-mail:
			☐ Acknowledgment ☐ Oath/Affirmation ☐ Jurat ☐ Other _____		Signature

Name, Phone #, address of witness	Signature of witness	Identity	Right Thumbprint	Notary / Travel Fee
		☐ Driver's license ☐ Credible Witness ☐ Passport ☐ Personally Known ☐ I D Card ☐ Other_____ ☐ I D. # _____		

123 Notary Public Record

Notarized Date/Time	Date of Document	Type of Documents	Service	Name, Phone #, address of signer	E-mail:
			☐ Acknowledgment ☐ Oath/Affirmation ☐ Jurat ☐ Other _____		Signature

Name, Phone #, address of witness	Signature of witness	Identity	Right Thumbprint	Notary / Travel Fee
		☐ Driver's license ☐ Credible Witness ☐ Passport ☐ Personally Known ☐ I D Card ☐ Other_____ ☐ I D. # _____		

124 Notary Public Record

Notarized Date/Time	Date of Document	Type of Documents	Service	Name, Phone #, address of signer	E-mail:
_____ _____	_____	_____	☐ Acknowledgment ☐ Oath/Affirmation ☐ Jurat ☐ Other _____	_____ _____ _____	Signature _____

Name, Phone #, address of witness	Signature of witness	Identity		Right Thumbprint	Notary / Travel Fee
_____ _____	_____	☐ Driver's license ☐ Credible Witness ☐ Passport ☐ Personally Known ☐ I D Card ☐ Other_____ ☐ I D. # _____			

125 Notary Public Record

Notarized Date/Time	Date of Document	Type of Documents	Service	Name, Phone #, address of signer	E-mail:
_____ _____	_____	_____	☐ Acknowledgment ☐ Oath/Affirmation ☐ Jurat ☐ Other _____	_____ _____ _____	Signature _____

Name, Phone #, address of witness	Signature of witness	Identity		Right Thumbprint	Notary / Travel Fee
_____ _____	_____	☐ Driver's license ☐ Credible Witness ☐ Passport ☐ Personally Known ☐ I D Card ☐ Other_____ ☐ I D. # _____			

126 Notary Public Record

Notarized Date/Time	Date of Document	Type of Documents	Service	Name, Phone #, address of signer	E-mail:
_____ _____	_____	_____	☐ Acknowledgment ☐ Oath/Affirmation ☐ Jurat ☐ Other _____	_____ _____ _____	Signature _____

Name, Phone #, address of witness	Signature of witness	Identity		Right Thumbprint	Notary / Travel Fee
_____ _____	_____	☐ Driver's license ☐ Credible Witness ☐ Passport ☐ Personally Known ☐ I D Card ☐ Other_____ ☐ I D. # _____			

127 Notary Public Record

Notarized Date/Time	Date of Document	Type of Documents	Service	Name, Phone #, address of signer	E-mail:
		_____	☐ Acknowledgment ☐ Oath/Affirmation ☐ Jurat ☐ Other _____	_____	Signature
_____	_____	_____		_____	_____

Name, Phone #, address of witness	Signature of witness	Identity	Right Thumbprint	Notary / Travel Fee
_____ _____		☐ Driver's license ☐ Credible Witness ☐ Passport ☐ Personally Known ☐ I D Card ☐ Other_____ ☐ I D. # _____		

128 Notary Public Record

Notarized Date/Time	Date of Document	Type of Documents	Service	Name, Phone #, address of signer	E-mail:
		_____	☐ Acknowledgment ☐ Oath/Affirmation ☐ Jurat ☐ Other _____	_____	Signature
_____	_____	_____		_____	_____

Name, Phone #, address of witness	Signature of witness	Identity	Right Thumbprint	Notary / Travel Fee
_____ _____		☐ Driver's license ☐ Credible Witness ☐ Passport ☐ Personally Known ☐ I D Card ☐ Other_____ ☐ I D. # _____		

129 Notary Public Record

Notarized Date/Time	Date of Document	Type of Documents	Service	Name, Phone #, address of signer	E-mail:
		_____	☐ Acknowledgment ☐ Oath/Affirmation ☐ Jurat ☐ Other _____	_____	Signature
_____	_____	_____		_____	_____

Name, Phone #, address of witness	Signature of witness	Identity	Right Thumbprint	Notary / Travel Fee
_____ _____		☐ Driver's license ☐ Credible Witness ☐ Passport ☐ Personally Known ☐ I D Card ☐ Other_____ ☐ I D. # _____		

Notary Public Record

130

Notarized Date/Time	Date of Document	Type of Documents	Service	Name, Phone #, address of signer	E-mail:
_____ _____	_____	_____ _____	☐ Acknowledgment ☐ Oath/Affirmation ☐ Jurat ☐ Other ————	_____ _____	Signature _____

Name, Phone #, address of witness	Signature of witness	Identity	Right Thumbprint	Notary / Travel Fee
_____		☐ Driver's license ☐ Credible Witness ☐ Passport ☐ Personally Known ☐ I D Card ☐ Other_____ ☐ I D. # _____		

Notary Public Record

131

Notarized Date/Time	Date of Document	Type of Documents	Service	Name, Phone #, address of signer	E-mail:
_____ _____	_____	_____ _____	☐ Acknowledgment ☐ Oath/Affirmation ☐ Jurat ☐ Other ————	_____ _____	Signature _____

Name, Phone #, address of witness	Signature of witness	Identity	Right Thumbprint	Notary / Travel Fee
_____		☐ Driver's license ☐ Credible Witness ☐ Passport ☐ Personally Known ☐ I D Card ☐ Other_____ ☐ I D. # _____		

Notary Public Record

132

Notarized Date/Time	Date of Document	Type of Documents	Service	Name, Phone #, address of signer	E-mail:
_____ _____	_____	_____ _____	☐ Acknowledgment ☐ Oath/Affirmation ☐ Jurat ☐ Other ————	_____ _____	Signature _____

Name, Phone #, address of witness	Signature of witness	Identity	Right Thumbprint	Notary / Travel Fee
_____		☐ Driver's license ☐ Credible Witness ☐ Passport ☐ Personally Known ☐ I D Card ☐ Other_____ ☐ I D. # _____		

133 Notary Public Record

Notarized Date/Time	Date of Document	Type of Documents	Service	Name, Phone #, address of signer	E-mail:
		_____	☐ Acknowledgment ☐ Oath/Affirmation ☐ Jurat ☐ Other _____	_____	Signature
_____	_____	_____		_____	_____
		_____		_____	

Name, Phone #, address of witness	Signature of witness	Identity	Right Thumbprint	Notary / Travel Fee
		☐ Driver's license ☐ Credible Witness ☐ Passport ☐ Personally Known ☐ I D Card ☐ Other_____		
		☐ I D. # _____		

134 Notary Public Record

Notarized Date/Time	Date of Document	Type of Documents	Service	Name, Phone #, address of signer	E-mail:
		_____	☐ Acknowledgment ☐ Oath/Affirmation ☐ Jurat ☐ Other _____	_____	Signature
_____	_____	_____		_____	_____
		_____		_____	

Name, Phone #, address of witness	Signature of witness	Identity	Right Thumbprint	Notary / Travel Fee
		☐ Driver's license ☐ Credible Witness ☐ Passport ☐ Personally Known ☐ I D Card ☐ Other_____		
		☐ I D. # _____		

135 Notary Public Record

Notarized Date/Time	Date of Document	Type of Documents	Service	Name, Phone #, address of signer	E-mail:
		_____	☐ Acknowledgment ☐ Oath/Affirmation ☐ Jurat ☐ Other _____	_____	Signature
_____	_____	_____		_____	_____
		_____		_____	

Name, Phone #, address of witness	Signature of witness	Identity	Right Thumbprint	Notary / Travel Fee
		☐ Driver's license ☐ Credible Witness ☐ Passport ☐ Personally Known ☐ I D Card ☐ Other_____		
		☐ I D. # _____		

136 Notary Public Record

Notarized Date/Time	Date of Document	Type of Documents	Service	Name, Phone #, address of signer	E-mail:
			☐ Acknowledgment ☐ Oath/Affirmation ☐ Jurat ☐ Other _____		Signature

Name, Phone #, address of witness	Signature of witness	Identity	Right Thumbprint	Notary / Travel Fee
		☐ Driver's license ☐ Credible Witness ☐ Passport ☐ Personally Known ☐ I D Card ☐ Other_____ ☐ I D. # _____		

137 Notary Public Record

Notarized Date/Time	Date of Document	Type of Documents	Service	Name, Phone #, address of signer	E-mail:
			☐ Acknowledgment ☐ Oath/Affirmation ☐ Jurat ☐ Other _____		Signature

Name, Phone #, address of witness	Signature of witness	Identity	Right Thumbprint	Notary / Travel Fee
		☐ Driver's license ☐ Credible Witness ☐ Passport ☐ Personally Known ☐ I D Card ☐ Other_____ ☐ I D. # _____		

138 Notary Public Record

Notarized Date/Time	Date of Document	Type of Documents	Service	Name, Phone #, address of signer	E-mail:
			☐ Acknowledgment ☐ Oath/Affirmation ☐ Jurat ☐ Other _____		Signature

Name, Phone #, address of witness	Signature of witness	Identity	Right Thumbprint	Notary / Travel Fee
		☐ Driver's license ☐ Credible Witness ☐ Passport ☐ Personally Known ☐ I D Card ☐ Other_____ ☐ I D. # _____		

139 Notary Public Record

Notarized Date/Time	Date of Document	Type of Documents	Service	Name, Phone #, address of signer	E-mail:
			☐ Acknowledgment ☐ Oath/Affirmation ☐ Jurat ☐ Other _____		Signature

Name, Phone #, address of witness	Signature of witness	Identity	Right Thumbprint	Notary / Travel Fee
		☐ Driver's license ☐ Credible Witness ☐ Passport ☐ Personally Known ☐ I D Card ☐ Other _____ ☐ I D. # _____		

140 Notary Public Record

Notarized Date/Time	Date of Document	Type of Documents	Service	Name, Phone #, address of signer	E-mail:
			☐ Acknowledgment ☐ Oath/Affirmation ☐ Jurat ☐ Other _____		Signature

Name, Phone #, address of witness	Signature of witness	Identity	Right Thumbprint	Notary / Travel Fee
		☐ Driver's license ☐ Credible Witness ☐ Passport ☐ Personally Known ☐ I D Card ☐ Other _____ ☐ I D. # _____		

141 Notary Public Record

Notarized Date/Time	Date of Document	Type of Documents	Service	Name, Phone #, address of signer	E-mail:
			☐ Acknowledgment ☐ Oath/Affirmation ☐ Jurat ☐ Other _____		Signature

Name, Phone #, address of witness	Signature of witness	Identity	Right Thumbprint	Notary / Travel Fee
		☐ Driver's license ☐ Credible Witness ☐ Passport ☐ Personally Known ☐ I D Card ☐ Other _____ ☐ I D. # _____		

142

Notary Public Record

Notarized Date/Time	Date of Document	Type of Documents	Service	Name, Phone #, address of signer	E-mail:
_____	_____	_____	☐ Acknowledgment ☐ Oath/Affirmation ☐ Jurat ☐ Other _____	_____	Signature
_____		_____		_____	_____

Name, Phone #, address of witness	Signature of witness	Identity	Right Thumbprint	Notary / Travel Fee
_____		☐ Driver's license ☐ Credible Witness ☐ Passport ☐ Personally Known ☐ I D Card ☐ Other_____ ☐ I D. # _____		

143

Notary Public Record

Notarized Date/Time	Date of Document	Type of Documents	Service	Name, Phone #, address of signer	E-mail:
_____	_____	_____	☐ Acknowledgment ☐ Oath/Affirmation ☐ Jurat ☐ Other _____	_____	Signature
_____		_____		_____	_____

Name, Phone #, address of witness	Signature of witness	Identity	Right Thumbprint	Notary / Travel Fee
_____		☐ Driver's license ☐ Credible Witness ☐ Passport ☐ Personally Known ☐ I D Card ☐ Other_____ ☐ I D. # _____		

144

Notary Public Record

Notarized Date/Time	Date of Document	Type of Documents	Service	Name, Phone #, address of signer	E-mail:
_____	_____	_____	☐ Acknowledgment ☐ Oath/Affirmation ☐ Jurat ☐ Other _____	_____	Signature
_____		_____		_____	_____

Name, Phone #, address of witness	Signature of witness	Identity	Right Thumbprint	Notary / Travel Fee
_____		☐ Driver's license ☐ Credible Witness ☐ Passport ☐ Personally Known ☐ I D Card ☐ Other_____ ☐ I D. # _____		

145 Notary Public Record

Notarized Date/Time	Date of Document	Type of Documents	Service	Name, Phone #, address of signer	E-mail:
		_____	☐ Acknowledgment ☐ Oath/Affirmation ☐ Jurat ☐ Other _____	_____	Signature _____
_____	_____	_____		_____	

Name, Phone #, address of witness	Signature of witness	Identity	Right Thumbprint	Notary / Travel Fee
_____		☐ Driver's license ☐ Credible Witness ☐ Passport ☐ Personally Known ☐ I D Card ☐ Other _____ ☐ I D. # _____		

146 Notary Public Record

Notarized Date/Time	Date of Document	Type of Documents	Service	Name, Phone #, address of signer	E-mail:
		_____	☐ Acknowledgment ☐ Oath/Affirmation ☐ Jurat ☐ Other _____	_____	Signature _____
_____	_____	_____		_____	

Name, Phone #, address of witness	Signature of witness	Identity	Right Thumbprint	Notary / Travel Fee
_____		☐ Driver's license ☐ Credible Witness ☐ Passport ☐ Personally Known ☐ I D Card ☐ Other _____ ☐ I D. # _____		

147 Notary Public Record

Notarized Date/Time	Date of Document	Type of Documents	Service	Name, Phone #, address of signer	E-mail:
		_____	☐ Acknowledgment ☐ Oath/Affirmation ☐ Jurat ☐ Other _____	_____	Signature _____
_____	_____	_____		_____	

Name, Phone #, address of witness	Signature of witness	Identity	Right Thumbprint	Notary / Travel Fee
_____		☐ Driver's license ☐ Credible Witness ☐ Passport ☐ Personally Known ☐ I D Card ☐ Other _____ ☐ I D. # _____		

148 Notary Public Record

Notarized Date/Time	Date of Document	Type of Documents	Service	Name, Phone #, address of signer	E-mail:
_____ _____	_____	_____	☐ Acknowledgment ☐ Oath/Affirmation ☐ Jurat ☐ Other _____	_____ _____	Signature

Name, Phone #, address of witness	Signature of witness	Identity		Right Thumbprint	Notary / Travel Fee
_____ _____		☐ Driver's license ☐ Credible Witness ☐ Passport ☐ Personally Known ☐ I D Card ☐ Other_____ ☐ I D. # _____			

149 Notary Public Record

Notarized Date/Time	Date of Document	Type of Documents	Service	Name, Phone #, address of signer	E-mail:
_____ _____	_____	_____	☐ Acknowledgment ☐ Oath/Affirmation ☐ Jurat ☐ Other _____	_____ _____	Signature

Name, Phone #, address of witness	Signature of witness	Identity		Right Thumbprint	Notary / Travel Fee
_____ _____		☐ Driver's license ☐ Credible Witness ☐ Passport ☐ Personally Known ☐ I D Card ☐ Other_____ ☐ I D. # _____			

150 Notary Public Record

Notarized Date/Time	Date of Document	Type of Documents	Service	Name, Phone #, address of signer	E-mail:
_____ _____	_____	_____	☐ Acknowledgment ☐ Oath/Affirmation ☐ Jurat ☐ Other _____	_____ _____	Signature

Name, Phone #, address of witness	Signature of witness	Identity		Right Thumbprint	Notary / Travel Fee
_____ _____		☐ Driver's license ☐ Credible Witness ☐ Passport ☐ Personally Known ☐ I D Card ☐ Other_____ ☐ I D. # _____			

151 Notary Public Record

Notarized Date/Time	Date of Document	Type of Documents	Service	Name, Phone #, address of signer	E-mail:
			☐ Acknowledgment ☐ Oath/Affirmation ☐ Jurat ☐ Other _____		Signature

Name, Phone #, address of witness	Signature of witness	Identity	Right Thumbprint	Notary / Travel Fee
		☐ Driver's license ☐ Credible Witness ☐ Passport ☐ Personally Known ☐ I D Card ☐ Other_____ ☐ I D. # _____		

152 Notary Public Record

Notarized Date/Time	Date of Document	Type of Documents	Service	Name, Phone #, address of signer	E-mail:
			☐ Acknowledgment ☐ Oath/Affirmation ☐ Jurat ☐ Other _____		Signature

Name, Phone #, address of witness	Signature of witness	Identity	Right Thumbprint	Notary / Travel Fee
		☐ Driver's license ☐ Credible Witness ☐ Passport ☐ Personally Known ☐ I D Card ☐ Other_____ ☐ I D. # _____		

153 Notary Public Record

Notarized Date/Time	Date of Document	Type of Documents	Service	Name, Phone #, address of signer	E-mail:
			☐ Acknowledgment ☐ Oath/Affirmation ☐ Jurat ☐ Other _____		Signature

Name, Phone #, address of witness	Signature of witness	Identity	Right Thumbprint	Notary / Travel Fee
		☐ Driver's license ☐ Credible Witness ☐ Passport ☐ Personally Known ☐ I D Card ☐ Other_____ ☐ I D. # _____		

154 Notary Public Record

Notarized Date/Time	Date of Document	Type of Documents	Service	Name, Phone #, address of signer	E-mail:
			☐ Acknowledgment ☐ Oath/Affirmation ☐ Jurat ☐ Other _____		Signature

Name, Phone #, address of witness	Signature of witness	Identity		Right Thumbprint	Notary / Travel Fee
		☐ Driver's license ☐ Credible Witness ☐ Passport ☐ Personally Known ☐ I D Card ☐ Other_____ ☐ I D. # _____			

155 Notary Public Record

Notarized Date/Time	Date of Document	Type of Documents	Service	Name, Phone #, address of signer	E-mail:
			☐ Acknowledgment ☐ Oath/Affirmation ☐ Jurat ☐ Other _____		Signature

Name, Phone #, address of witness	Signature of witness	Identity		Right Thumbprint	Notary / Travel Fee
		☐ Driver's license ☐ Credible Witness ☐ Passport ☐ Personally Known ☐ I D Card ☐ Other_____ ☐ I D. # _____			

156 Notary Public Record

Notarized Date/Time	Date of Document	Type of Documents	Service	Name, Phone #, address of signer	E-mail:
			☐ Acknowledgment ☐ Oath/Affirmation ☐ Jurat ☐ Other _____		Signature

Name, Phone #, address of witness	Signature of witness	Identity		Right Thumbprint	Notary / Travel Fee
		☐ Driver's license ☐ Credible Witness ☐ Passport ☐ Personally Known ☐ I D Card ☐ Other_____ ☐ I D. # _____			

157 Notary Public Record

Notarized Date/Time	Date of Document	Type of Documents	Service	Name, Phone #, address of signer	E-mail:
			☐ Acknowledgment ☐ Oath/Affirmation ☐ Jurat ☐ Other _____		Signature

Name, Phone #, address of witness	Signature of witness	Identity	Right Thumbprint	Notary / Travel Fee
		☐ Driver's license ☐ Credible Witness ☐ Passport ☐ Personally Known ☐ I D Card ☐ Other_____ ☐ I D. # _____		

158 Notary Public Record

Notarized Date/Time	Date of Document	Type of Documents	Service	Name, Phone #, address of signer	E-mail:
			☐ Acknowledgment ☐ Oath/Affirmation ☐ Jurat ☐ Other _____		Signature

Name, Phone #, address of witness	Signature of witness	Identity	Right Thumbprint	Notary / Travel Fee
		☐ Driver's license ☐ Credible Witness ☐ Passport ☐ Personally Known ☐ I D Card ☐ Other_____ ☐ I D. # _____		

159 Notary Public Record

Notarized Date/Time	Date of Document	Type of Documents	Service	Name, Phone #, address of signer	E-mail:
			☐ Acknowledgment ☐ Oath/Affirmation ☐ Jurat ☐ Other _____		Signature

Name, Phone #, address of witness	Signature of witness	Identity	Right Thumbprint	Notary / Travel Fee
		☐ Driver's license ☐ Credible Witness ☐ Passport ☐ Personally Known ☐ I D Card ☐ Other_____ ☐ I D. # _____		

160 Notary Public Record

Notarized Date/Time	Date of Document	Type of Documents	Service	Name, Phone #, address of signer	E-mail:
_____ _____	_____	_____ _____ _____	☐ Acknowledgment ☐ Oath/Affirmation ☐ Jurat ☐ Other _____	_____ _____	Signature _____

Name, Phone #, address of witness	Signature of witness	Identity		Right Thumbprint	Notary / Travel Fee
_____ _____		☐ Driver's license ☐ Credible Witness ☐ Passport ☐ Personally Known ☐ I D Card ☐ Other_____ ☐ I D. # _____			

161 Notary Public Record

Notarized Date/Time	Date of Document	Type of Documents	Service	Name, Phone #, address of signer	E-mail:
_____ _____	_____	_____ _____ _____	☐ Acknowledgment ☐ Oath/Affirmation ☐ Jurat ☐ Other _____	_____ _____	Signature _____

Name, Phone #, address of witness	Signature of witness	Identity		Right Thumbprint	Notary / Travel Fee
_____ _____		☐ Driver's license ☐ Credible Witness ☐ Passport ☐ Personally Known ☐ I D Card ☐ Other_____ ☐ I D. # _____			

162 Notary Public Record

Notarized Date/Time	Date of Document	Type of Documents	Service	Name, Phone #, address of signer	E-mail:
_____ _____	_____	_____ _____ _____	☐ Acknowledgment ☐ Oath/Affirmation ☐ Jurat ☐ Other _____	_____ _____	Signature _____

Name, Phone #, address of witness	Signature of witness	Identity		Right Thumbprint	Notary / Travel Fee
_____ _____		☐ Driver's license ☐ Credible Witness ☐ Passport ☐ Personally Known ☐ I D Card ☐ Other_____ ☐ I D. # _____			

163 Notary Public Record

Notarized Date/Time	Date of Document	Type of Documents	Service	Name, Phone #, address of signer	E-mail:
			☐ Acknowledgment ☐ Oath/Affirmation ☐ Jurat ☐ Other _____		Signature

Name, Phone #, address of witness	Signature of witness	Identity	Right Thumbprint	Notary / Travel Fee
		☐ Driver's license ☐ Credible Witness ☐ Passport ☐ Personally Known ☐ I D Card ☐ Other_____ ☐ I D. # _____		

164 Notary Public Record

Notarized Date/Time	Date of Document	Type of Documents	Service	Name, Phone #, address of signer	E-mail:
			☐ Acknowledgment ☐ Oath/Affirmation ☐ Jurat ☐ Other _____		Signature

Name, Phone #, address of witness	Signature of witness	Identity	Right Thumbprint	Notary / Travel Fee
		☐ Driver's license ☐ Credible Witness ☐ Passport ☐ Personally Known ☐ I D Card ☐ Other_____ ☐ I D. # _____		

165 Notary Public Record

Notarized Date/Time	Date of Document	Type of Documents	Service	Name, Phone #, address of signer	E-mail:
			☐ Acknowledgment ☐ Oath/Affirmation ☐ Jurat ☐ Other _____		Signature

Name, Phone #, address of witness	Signature of witness	Identity	Right Thumbprint	Notary / Travel Fee
		☐ Driver's license ☐ Credible Witness ☐ Passport ☐ Personally Known ☐ I D Card ☐ Other_____ ☐ I D. # _____		

166 Notary Public Record

Notarized Date/Time	Date of Document	Type of Documents	Service	Name, Phone #, address of signer	E-mail:
			☐ Acknowledgment ☐ Oath/Affirmation ☐ Jurat ☐ Other _____		Signature

Name, Phone #, address of witness	Signature of witness	Identity	Right Thumbprint	Notary / Travel Fee
		☐ Driver's license ☐ Credible Witness ☐ Passport ☐ Personally Known ☐ I D Card ☐ Other_____ ☐ I D. # _____		

167 Notary Public Record

Notarized Date/Time	Date of Document	Type of Documents	Service	Name, Phone #, address of signer	E-mail:
			☐ Acknowledgment ☐ Oath/Affirmation ☐ Jurat ☐ Other _____		Signature

Name, Phone #, address of witness	Signature of witness	Identity	Right Thumbprint	Notary / Travel Fee
		☐ Driver's license ☐ Credible Witness ☐ Passport ☐ Personally Known ☐ I D Card ☐ Other_____ ☐ I D. # _____		

168 Notary Public Record

Notarized Date/Time	Date of Document	Type of Documents	Service	Name, Phone #, address of signer	E-mail:
			☐ Acknowledgment ☐ Oath/Affirmation ☐ Jurat ☐ Other _____		Signature

Name, Phone #, address of witness	Signature of witness	Identity	Right Thumbprint	Notary / Travel Fee
		☐ Driver's license ☐ Credible Witness ☐ Passport ☐ Personally Known ☐ I D Card ☐ Other_____ ☐ I D. # _____		

169 Notary Public Record

Notarized Date/Time	Date of Document	Type of Documents	Service	Name, Phone #, address of signer	E-mail:
			☐ Acknowledgment ☐ Oath/Affirmation ☐ Jurat ☐ Other _____		Signature

Name, Phone #, address of witness	Signature of witness	Identity	Right Thumbprint	Notary / Travel Fee
		☐ Driver's license ☐ Credible Witness ☐ Passport ☐ Personally Known ☐ I D Card ☐ Other _____ ☐ I D. # _____		

170 Notary Public Record

Notarized Date/Time	Date of Document	Type of Documents	Service	Name, Phone #, address of signer	E-mail:
			☐ Acknowledgment ☐ Oath/Affirmation ☐ Jurat ☐ Other _____		Signature

Name, Phone #, address of witness	Signature of witness	Identity	Right Thumbprint	Notary / Travel Fee
		☐ Driver's license ☐ Credible Witness ☐ Passport ☐ Personally Known ☐ I D Card ☐ Other _____ ☐ I D. # _____		

171 Notary Public Record

Notarized Date/Time	Date of Document	Type of Documents	Service	Name, Phone #, address of signer	E-mail:
			☐ Acknowledgment ☐ Oath/Affirmation ☐ Jurat ☐ Other _____		Signature

Name, Phone #, address of witness	Signature of witness	Identity	Right Thumbprint	Notary / Travel Fee
		☐ Driver's license ☐ Credible Witness ☐ Passport ☐ Personally Known ☐ I D Card ☐ Other _____ ☐ I D. # _____		

172 Notary Public Record

Notarized Date/Time	Date of Document	Type of Documents	Service	Name, Phone #, address of signer	E-mail:
			☐ Acknowledgment ☐ Oath/Affirmation ☐ Jurat ☐ Other _____		Signature

Name, Phone #, address of witness	Signature of witness	Identity	Right Thumbprint	Notary / Travel Fee
		☐ Driver's license ☐ Credible Witness ☐ Passport ☐ Personally Known ☐ I D Card ☐ Other_____ ☐ I D. # _____		

173 Notary Public Record

Notarized Date/Time	Date of Document	Type of Documents	Service	Name, Phone #, address of signer	E-mail:
			☐ Acknowledgment ☐ Oath/Affirmation ☐ Jurat ☐ Other _____		Signature

Name, Phone #, address of witness	Signature of witness	Identity	Right Thumbprint	Notary / Travel Fee
		☐ Driver's license ☐ Credible Witness ☐ Passport ☐ Personally Known ☐ I D Card ☐ Other_____ ☐ I D. # _____		

174 Notary Public Record

Notarized Date/Time	Date of Document	Type of Documents	Service	Name, Phone #, address of signer	E-mail:
			☐ Acknowledgment ☐ Oath/Affirmation ☐ Jurat ☐ Other _____		Signature

Name, Phone #, address of witness	Signature of witness	Identity	Right Thumbprint	Notary / Travel Fee
		☐ Driver's license ☐ Credible Witness ☐ Passport ☐ Personally Known ☐ I D Card ☐ Other_____ ☐ I D. # _____		

Notary Public Record

175

Notarized Date/Time	Date of Document	Type of Documents	Service	Name, Phone #, address of signer	E-mail:
		_____	☐ Acknowledgment ☐ Oath/Affirmation ☐ Jurat ☐ Other _____	_____	Signature
_____	_____	_____		_____	_____

Name, Phone #, address of witness	Signature of witness	Identity	Right Thumbprint	Notary / Travel Fee
_____		☐ Driver's license ☐ Credible Witness ☐ Passport ☐ Personally Known ☐ I D Card ☐ Other_____ ☐ I D. # _____		

Notary Public Record

176

Notarized Date/Time	Date of Document	Type of Documents	Service	Name, Phone #, address of signer	E-mail:
		_____	☐ Acknowledgment ☐ Oath/Affirmation ☐ Jurat ☐ Other _____	_____	Signature
_____	_____	_____		_____	_____

Name, Phone #, address of witness	Signature of witness	Identity	Right Thumbprint	Notary / Travel Fee
_____		☐ Driver's license ☐ Credible Witness ☐ Passport ☐ Personally Known ☐ I D Card ☐ Other_____ ☐ I D. # _____		

Notary Public Record

177

Notarized Date/Time	Date of Document	Type of Documents	Service	Name, Phone #, address of signer	E-mail:
		_____	☐ Acknowledgment ☐ Oath/Affirmation ☐ Jurat ☐ Other _____	_____	Signature
_____	_____	_____		_____	_____

Name, Phone #, address of witness	Signature of witness	Identity	Right Thumbprint	Notary / Travel Fee
_____		☐ Driver's license ☐ Credible Witness ☐ Passport ☐ Personally Known ☐ I D Card ☐ Other_____ ☐ I D. # _____		

178 Notary Public Record

Notarized Date/Time	Date of Document	Type of Documents	Service	Name, Phone #, address of signer	E-mail:
			☐ Acknowledgment ☐ Oath/Affirmation ☐ Jurat ☐ Other		Signature

Name, Phone #, address of witness	Signature of witness	Identity	Right Thumbprint	Notary / Travel Fee
		☐ Driver's license ☐ Credible Witness ☐ Passport ☐ Personally Known ☐ I D Card ☐ Other_____ ☐ I D. #_____		

179 Notary Public Record

Notarized Date/Time	Date of Document	Type of Documents	Service	Name, Phone #, address of signer	E-mail:
			☐ Acknowledgment ☐ Oath/Affirmation ☐ Jurat ☐ Other		Signature

Name, Phone #, address of witness	Signature of witness	Identity	Right Thumbprint	Notary / Travel Fee
		☐ Driver's license ☐ Credible Witness ☐ Passport ☐ Personally Known ☐ I D Card ☐ Other_____ ☐ I D. #_____		

180 Notary Public Record

Notarized Date/Time	Date of Document	Type of Documents	Service	Name, Phone #, address of signer	E-mail:
			☐ Acknowledgment ☐ Oath/Affirmation ☐ Jurat ☐ Other		Signature

Name, Phone #, address of witness	Signature of witness	Identity	Right Thumbprint	Notary / Travel Fee
		☐ Driver's license ☐ Credible Witness ☐ Passport ☐ Personally Known ☐ I D Card ☐ Other_____ ☐ I D. #_____		

181   *Notary Public Record*

Notarized Date/Time	Date of Document	Type of Documents	Service	Name, Phone #, address of signer	E-mail:
			☐ Acknowledgment ☐ Oath/Affirmation ☐ Jurat ☐ Other _____		Signature

Name, Phone #, address of witness	Signature of witness	Identity	Right Thumbprint	Notary / Travel Fee
		☐ Driver's license ☐ Credible Witness ☐ Passport ☐ Personally Known ☐ I D Card ☐ Other_____ ☐ I D. # _____		

182   *Notary Public Record*

Notarized Date/Time	Date of Document	Type of Documents	Service	Name, Phone #, address of signer	E-mail:
			☐ Acknowledgment ☐ Oath/Affirmation ☐ Jurat ☐ Other _____		Signature

Name, Phone #, address of witness	Signature of witness	Identity	Right Thumbprint	Notary / Travel Fee
		☐ Driver's license ☐ Credible Witness ☐ Passport ☐ Personally Known ☐ I D Card ☐ Other_____ ☐ I D. # _____		

183   *Notary Public Record*

Notarized Date/Time	Date of Document	Type of Documents	Service	Name, Phone #, address of signer	E-mail:
			☐ Acknowledgment ☐ Oath/Affirmation ☐ Jurat ☐ Other _____		Signature

Name, Phone #, address of witness	Signature of witness	Identity	Right Thumbprint	Notary / Travel Fee
		☐ Driver's license ☐ Credible Witness ☐ Passport ☐ Personally Known ☐ I D Card ☐ Other_____ ☐ I D. # _____		

184 Notary Public Record

Notarized Date/Time	Date of Document	Type of Documents	Service	Name, Phone #, address of signer	E-mail:
			☐ Acknowledgment ☐ Oath/Affirmation ☐ Jurat ☐ Other _____		Signature

Name, Phone #, address of witness	Signature of witness	Identity		Right Thumbprint	Notary / Travel Fee
		☐ Driver's license ☐ Credible Witness ☐ Passport ☐ Personally Known ☐ I D Card ☐ Other_____ ☐ I D. # _____			

185 Notary Public Record

Notarized Date/Time	Date of Document	Type of Documents	Service	Name, Phone #, address of signer	E-mail:
			☐ Acknowledgment ☐ Oath/Affirmation ☐ Jurat ☐ Other _____		Signature

Name, Phone #, address of witness	Signature of witness	Identity		Right Thumbprint	Notary / Travel Fee
		☐ Driver's license ☐ Credible Witness ☐ Passport ☐ Personally Known ☐ I D Card ☐ Other_____ ☐ I D. # _____			

186 Notary Public Record

Notarized Date/Time	Date of Document	Type of Documents	Service	Name, Phone #, address of signer	E-mail:
			☐ Acknowledgment ☐ Oath/Affirmation ☐ Jurat ☐ Other _____		Signature

Name, Phone #, address of witness	Signature of witness	Identity		Right Thumbprint	Notary / Travel Fee
		☐ Driver's license ☐ Credible Witness ☐ Passport ☐ Personally Known ☐ I D Card ☐ Other_____ ☐ I D. # _____			

187 Notary Public Record

Notarized Date/Time	Date of Document	Type of Documents	Service	Name, Phone #, address of signer	E-mail:
		_____	☐ Acknowledgment ☐ Oath/Affirmation ☐ Jurat ☐ Other _____	_____	Signature
		_____		_____	_____

Name, Phone #, address of witness	Signature of witness	Identity	Right Thumbprint	Notary / Travel Fee
		☐ Driver's license ☐ Credible Witness ☐ Passport ☐ Personally Known ☐ I D Card ☐ Other_____ ☐ I D. # _____		

188 Notary Public Record

Notarized Date/Time	Date of Document	Type of Documents	Service	Name, Phone #, address of signer	E-mail:
		_____	☐ Acknowledgment ☐ Oath/Affirmation ☐ Jurat ☐ Other _____	_____	Signature
		_____		_____	_____

Name, Phone #, address of witness	Signature of witness	Identity	Right Thumbprint	Notary / Travel Fee
		☐ Driver's license ☐ Credible Witness ☐ Passport ☐ Personally Known ☐ I D Card ☐ Other_____ ☐ I D. # _____		

189 Notary Public Record

Notarized Date/Time	Date of Document	Type of Documents	Service	Name, Phone #, address of signer	E-mail:
		_____	☐ Acknowledgment ☐ Oath/Affirmation ☐ Jurat ☐ Other _____	_____	Signature
		_____		_____	_____

Name, Phone #, address of witness	Signature of witness	Identity	Right Thumbprint	Notary / Travel Fee
		☐ Driver's license ☐ Credible Witness ☐ Passport ☐ Personally Known ☐ I D Card ☐ Other_____ ☐ I D. # _____		

190 Notary Public Record

Notarized Date/Time	Date of Document	Type of Documents	Service	Name, Phone #, address of signer	E-mail:
			☐ Acknowledgment ☐ Oath/Affirmation ☐ Jurat ☐ Other ———		Signature

Name, Phone #, address of witness	Signature of witness	Identity	Right Thumbprint	Notary / Travel Fee
		☐ Driver's license ☐ Credible Witness ☐ Passport ☐ Personally Known ☐ I D Card ☐ Other_____ ☐ I D. # _____		

191 Notary Public Record

Notarized Date/Time	Date of Document	Type of Documents	Service	Name, Phone #, address of signer	E-mail:
			☐ Acknowledgment ☐ Oath/Affirmation ☐ Jurat ☐ Other ———		Signature

Name, Phone #, address of witness	Signature of witness	Identity	Right Thumbprint	Notary / Travel Fee
		☐ Driver's license ☐ Credible Witness ☐ Passport ☐ Personally Known ☐ I D Card ☐ Other_____ ☐ I D. # _____		

192 Notary Public Record

Notarized Date/Time	Date of Document	Type of Documents	Service	Name, Phone #, address of signer	E-mail:
			☐ Acknowledgment ☐ Oath/Affirmation ☐ Jurat ☐ Other ———		Signature

Name, Phone #, address of witness	Signature of witness	Identity	Right Thumbprint	Notary / Travel Fee
		☐ Driver's license ☐ Credible Witness ☐ Passport ☐ Personally Known ☐ I D Card ☐ Other_____ ☐ I D. # _____		

193 Notary Public Record

Notarized Date/Time	Date of Document	Type of Documents	Service	Name, Phone #, address of signer	E-mail:
			☐ Acknowledgment ☐ Oath/Affirmation ☐ Jurat ☐ Other _____		Signature

Name, Phone #, address of witness	Signature of witness	Identity	Right Thumbprint	Notary / Travel Fee
		☐ Driver's license ☐ Credible Witness ☐ Passport ☐ Personally Known ☐ I D Card ☐ Other_____ ☐ I D. # _____		

194 Notary Public Record

Notarized Date/Time	Date of Document	Type of Documents	Service	Name, Phone #, address of signer	E-mail:
			☐ Acknowledgment ☐ Oath/Affirmation ☐ Jurat ☐ Other _____		Signature

Name, Phone #, address of witness	Signature of witness	Identity	Right Thumbprint	Notary / Travel Fee
		☐ Driver's license ☐ Credible Witness ☐ Passport ☐ Personally Known ☐ I D Card ☐ Other_____ ☐ I D. # _____		

195 Notary Public Record

Notarized Date/Time	Date of Document	Type of Documents	Service	Name, Phone #, address of signer	E-mail:
			☐ Acknowledgment ☐ Oath/Affirmation ☐ Jurat ☐ Other _____		Signature

Name, Phone #, address of witness	Signature of witness	Identity	Right Thumbprint	Notary / Travel Fee
		☐ Driver's license ☐ Credible Witness ☐ Passport ☐ Personally Known ☐ I D Card ☐ Other_____ ☐ I D. # _____		

196 Notary Public Record

Notarized Date/Time	Date of Document	Type of Documents	Service	Name, Phone #, address of signer	E-mail:
_____ _____	_____	_____ _____ _____	☐ Acknowledgment ☐ Oath/Affirmation ☐ Jurat ☐ Other _____	_____ _____ _____	Signature

Name, Phone #, address of witness	Signature of witness	Identity	Right Thumbprint	Notary / Travel Fee
_____ _____		☐ Driver's license ☐ Credible Witness ☐ Passport ☐ Personally Known ☐ I D Card ☐ Other_____ ☐ I D. # _____		

197 Notary Public Record

Notarized Date/Time	Date of Document	Type of Documents	Service	Name, Phone #, address of signer	E-mail:
_____ _____	_____	_____ _____ _____	☐ Acknowledgment ☐ Oath/Affirmation ☐ Jurat ☐ Other _____	_____ _____ _____	Signature

Name, Phone #, address of witness	Signature of witness	Identity	Right Thumbprint	Notary / Travel Fee
_____ _____		☐ Driver's license ☐ Credible Witness ☐ Passport ☐ Personally Known ☐ I D Card ☐ Other_____ ☐ I D. # _____		

198 Notary Public Record

Notarized Date/Time	Date of Document	Type of Documents	Service	Name, Phone #, address of signer	E-mail:
_____ _____	_____	_____ _____ _____	☐ Acknowledgment ☐ Oath/Affirmation ☐ Jurat ☐ Other _____	_____ _____ _____	Signature

Name, Phone #, address of witness	Signature of witness	Identity	Right Thumbprint	Notary / Travel Fee
_____ _____		☐ Driver's license ☐ Credible Witness ☐ Passport ☐ Personally Known ☐ I D Card ☐ Other_____ ☐ I D. # _____		

199   *Notary Public Record*

Notarized Date/Time	Date of Document	Type of Documents	Service	Name, Phone #, address of signer	E-mail:
			☐ Acknowledgment ☐ Oath/Affirmation ☐ Jurat ☐ Other _____		Signature

Name, Phone #, address of witness	Signature of witness	Identity	Right Thumbprint	Notary / Travel Fee
		☐ Driver's license ☐ Credible Witness ☐ Passport ☐ Personally Known ☐ I D Card ☐ Other_____ ☐ I D. # _____		

200   *Notary Public Record*

Notarized Date/Time	Date of Document	Type of Documents	Service	Name, Phone #, address of signer	E-mail:
			☐ Acknowledgment ☐ Oath/Affirmation ☐ Jurat ☐ Other _____		Signature

Name, Phone #, address of witness	Signature of witness	Identity	Right Thumbprint	Notary / Travel Fee
		☐ Driver's license ☐ Credible Witness ☐ Passport ☐ Personally Known ☐ I D Card ☐ Other_____ ☐ I D. # _____		

201   *Notary Public Record*

Notarized Date/Time	Date of Document	Type of Documents	Service	Name, Phone #, address of signer	E-mail:
			☐ Acknowledgment ☐ Oath/Affirmation ☐ Jurat ☐ Other _____		Signature

Name, Phone #, address of witness	Signature of witness	Identity	Right Thumbprint	Notary / Travel Fee
		☐ Driver's license ☐ Credible Witness ☐ Passport ☐ Personally Known ☐ I D Card ☐ Other_____ ☐ I D. # _____		

202 Notary Public Record

Notarized Date/Time	Date of Document	Type of Documents	Service	Name, Phone #, address of signer	E-mail:
			☐ Acknowledgment ☐ Oath/Affirmation ☐ Jurat ☐ Other _____		Signature

Name, Phone #, address of witness	Signature of witness	Identity		Right Thumbprint	Notary / Travel Fee
		☐ Driver's license ☐ Credible Witness ☐ Passport ☐ Personally Known ☐ I D Card ☐ Other_____ ☐ I D. # _____			

203 Notary Public Record

Notarized Date/Time	Date of Document	Type of Documents	Service	Name, Phone #, address of signer	E-mail:
			☐ Acknowledgment ☐ Oath/Affirmation ☐ Jurat ☐ Other _____		Signature

Name, Phone #, address of witness	Signature of witness	Identity		Right Thumbprint	Notary / Travel Fee
		☐ Driver's license ☐ Credible Witness ☐ Passport ☐ Personally Known ☐ I D Card ☐ Other_____ ☐ I D. # _____			

204 Notary Public Record

Notarized Date/Time	Date of Document	Type of Documents	Service	Name, Phone #, address of signer	E-mail:
			☐ Acknowledgment ☐ Oath/Affirmation ☐ Jurat ☐ Other _____		Signature

Name, Phone #, address of witness	Signature of witness	Identity		Right Thumbprint	Notary / Travel Fee
		☐ Driver's license ☐ Credible Witness ☐ Passport ☐ Personally Known ☐ I D Card ☐ Other_____ ☐ I D. # _____			

205 — Notary Public Record

Notarized Date/Time	Date of Document	Type of Documents	Service	Name, Phone #, address of signer	E-mail:
			☐ Acknowledgment ☐ Oath/Affirmation ☐ Jurat ☐ Other _____		Signature

Name, Phone #, address of witness	Signature of witness	Identity	Right Thumbprint	Notary / Travel Fee
		☐ Driver's license ☐ Credible Witness ☐ Passport ☐ Personally Known ☐ I D Card ☐ Other_____ ☐ I D. # _____		

206 — Notary Public Record

Notarized Date/Time	Date of Document	Type of Documents	Service	Name, Phone #, address of signer	E-mail:
			☐ Acknowledgment ☐ Oath/Affirmation ☐ Jurat ☐ Other _____		Signature

Name, Phone #, address of witness	Signature of witness	Identity	Right Thumbprint	Notary / Travel Fee
		☐ Driver's license ☐ Credible Witness ☐ Passport ☐ Personally Known ☐ I D Card ☐ Other_____ ☐ I D. # _____		

207 — Notary Public Record

Notarized Date/Time	Date of Document	Type of Documents	Service	Name, Phone #, address of signer	E-mail:
			☐ Acknowledgment ☐ Oath/Affirmation ☐ Jurat ☐ Other _____		Signature

Name, Phone #, address of witness	Signature of witness	Identity	Right Thumbprint	Notary / Travel Fee
		☐ Driver's license ☐ Credible Witness ☐ Passport ☐ Personally Known ☐ I D Card ☐ Other_____ ☐ I D. # _____		

208 Notary Public Record

Notarized Date/Time	Date of Document	Type of Documents	Service	Name, Phone #, address of signer	E-mail:
_____ _____	_____	_____ _____	☐ Acknowledgment ☐ Oath/Affirmation ☐ Jurat ☐ Other _____	_____ _____ _____	Signature _____

Name, Phone #, address of witness	Signature of witness	Identity	Right Thumbprint	Notary / Travel Fee
_____ _____ _____	_____ _____	☐ Driver's license ☐ Credible Witness ☐ Passport ☐ Personally Known ☐ I D Card ☐ Other_____ ☐ I D. # _____		

209 Notary Public Record

Notarized Date/Time	Date of Document	Type of Documents	Service	Name, Phone #, address of signer	E-mail:
_____ _____	_____	_____ _____	☐ Acknowledgment ☐ Oath/Affirmation ☐ Jurat ☐ Other _____	_____ _____ _____	Signature _____

Name, Phone #, address of witness	Signature of witness	Identity	Right Thumbprint	Notary / Travel Fee
_____ _____ _____	_____ _____	☐ Driver's license ☐ Credible Witness ☐ Passport ☐ Personally Known ☐ I D Card ☐ Other_____ ☐ I D. # _____		

210 Notary Public Record

Notarized Date/Time	Date of Document	Type of Documents	Service	Name, Phone #, address of signer	E-mail:
_____ _____	_____	_____ _____	☐ Acknowledgment ☐ Oath/Affirmation ☐ Jurat ☐ Other _____	_____ _____ _____	Signature _____

Name, Phone #, address of witness	Signature of witness	Identity	Right Thumbprint	Notary / Travel Fee
_____ _____ _____	_____ _____	☐ Driver's license ☐ Credible Witness ☐ Passport ☐ Personally Known ☐ I D Card ☐ Other_____ ☐ I D. # _____		

211 Notary Public Record

Notarized Date/Time	Date of Document	Type of Documents	Service	Name, Phone #, address of signer	E-mail:
			☐ Acknowledgment ☐ Oath/Affirmation ☐ Jurat ☐ Other _____		Signature

Name, Phone #, address of witness	Signature of witness	Identity	Right Thumbprint	Notary / Travel Fee
		☐ Driver's license ☐ Credible Witness ☐ Passport ☐ Personally Known ☐ I D Card ☐ Other_____ ☐ I D. # _____		

212 Notary Public Record

Notarized Date/Time	Date of Document	Type of Documents	Service	Name, Phone #, address of signer	E-mail:
			☐ Acknowledgment ☐ Oath/Affirmation ☐ Jurat ☐ Other _____		Signature

Name, Phone #, address of witness	Signature of witness	Identity	Right Thumbprint	Notary / Travel Fee
		☐ Driver's license ☐ Credible Witness ☐ Passport ☐ Personally Known ☐ I D Card ☐ Other_____ ☐ I D. # _____		

213 Notary Public Record

Notarized Date/Time	Date of Document	Type of Documents	Service	Name, Phone #, address of signer	E-mail:
			☐ Acknowledgment ☐ Oath/Affirmation ☐ Jurat ☐ Other _____		Signature

Name, Phone #, address of witness	Signature of witness	Identity	Right Thumbprint	Notary / Travel Fee
		☐ Driver's license ☐ Credible Witness ☐ Passport ☐ Personally Known ☐ I D Card ☐ Other_____ ☐ I D. # _____		

214

Notary Public Record

Notarized Date/Time	Date of Document	Type of Documents	Service	Name, Phone #, address of signer	E-mail:
			☐ Acknowledgment ☐ Oath/Affirmation ☐ Jurat ☐ Other _____		Signature

Name, Phone #, address of witness	Signature of witness	Identity	Right Thumbprint	Notary / Travel Fee
		☐ Driver's license ☐ Credible Witness ☐ Passport ☐ Personally Known ☐ I D Card ☐ Other_____ ☐ I D. # _____		

215

Notary Public Record

Notarized Date/Time	Date of Document	Type of Documents	Service	Name, Phone #, address of signer	E-mail:
			☐ Acknowledgment ☐ Oath/Affirmation ☐ Jurat ☐ Other _____		Signature

Name, Phone #, address of witness	Signature of witness	Identity	Right Thumbprint	Notary / Travel Fee
		☐ Driver's license ☐ Credible Witness ☐ Passport ☐ Personally Known ☐ I D Card ☐ Other_____ ☐ I D. # _____		

216

Notary Public Record

Notarized Date/Time	Date of Document	Type of Documents	Service	Name, Phone #, address of signer	E-mail:
			☐ Acknowledgment ☐ Oath/Affirmation ☐ Jurat ☐ Other _____		Signature

Name, Phone #, address of witness	Signature of witness	Identity	Right Thumbprint	Notary / Travel Fee
		☐ Driver's license ☐ Credible Witness ☐ Passport ☐ Personally Known ☐ I D Card ☐ Other_____ ☐ I D. # _____		

217 Notary Public Record

Notarized Date/Time	Date of Document	Type of Documents	Service	Name, Phone #, address of signer	E-mail:
		_____	☐ Acknowledgment ☐ Oath/Affirmation ☐ Jurat ☐ Other _____	_____	Signature
_____	_____	_____		_____	
		_____		_____	_____

Name, Phone #, address of witness	Signature of witness	Identity	Right Thumbprint	Notary / Travel Fee
_____		☐ Driver's license ☐ Credible Witness ☐ Passport ☐ Personally Known ☐ I D Card ☐ Other_____		
_____		☐ I D. # _____		

218 Notary Public Record

Notarized Date/Time	Date of Document	Type of Documents	Service	Name, Phone #, address of signer	E-mail:
		_____	☐ Acknowledgment ☐ Oath/Affirmation ☐ Jurat ☐ Other _____	_____	Signature
_____	_____	_____		_____	
		_____		_____	_____

Name, Phone #, address of witness	Signature of witness	Identity	Right Thumbprint	Notary / Travel Fee
_____		☐ Driver's license ☐ Credible Witness ☐ Passport ☐ Personally Known ☐ I D Card ☐ Other_____		
_____		☐ I D. # _____		

219 Notary Public Record

Notarized Date/Time	Date of Document	Type of Documents	Service	Name, Phone #, address of signer	E-mail:
		_____	☐ Acknowledgment ☐ Oath/Affirmation ☐ Jurat ☐ Other _____	_____	Signature
_____	_____	_____		_____	
		_____		_____	_____

Name, Phone #, address of witness	Signature of witness	Identity	Right Thumbprint	Notary / Travel Fee
_____		☐ Driver's license ☐ Credible Witness ☐ Passport ☐ Personally Known ☐ I D Card ☐ Other_____		
_____		☐ I D. # _____		

220 Notary Public Record

Notarized Date/Time	Date of Document	Type of Documents	Service	Name, Phone #, address of signer	E-mail:
			☐ Acknowledgment ☐ Oath/Affirmation ☐ Jurat ☐ Other _____		Signature

Name, Phone #, address of witness	Signature of witness	Identity	Right Thumbprint	Notary / Travel Fee
		☐ Driver's license ☐ Credible Witness ☐ Passport ☐ Personally Known ☐ I D Card ☐ Other_____ ☐ I D. # _____		

221 Notary Public Record

Notarized Date/Time	Date of Document	Type of Documents	Service	Name, Phone #, address of signer	E-mail:
			☐ Acknowledgment ☐ Oath/Affirmation ☐ Jurat ☐ Other _____		Signature

Name, Phone #, address of witness	Signature of witness	Identity	Right Thumbprint	Notary / Travel Fee
		☐ Driver's license ☐ Credible Witness ☐ Passport ☐ Personally Known ☐ I D Card ☐ Other_____ ☐ I D. # _____		

222 Notary Public Record

Notarized Date/Time	Date of Document	Type of Documents	Service	Name, Phone #, address of signer	E-mail:
			☐ Acknowledgment ☐ Oath/Affirmation ☐ Jurat ☐ Other _____		Signature

Name, Phone #, address of witness	Signature of witness	Identity	Right Thumbprint	Notary / Travel Fee
		☐ Driver's license ☐ Credible Witness ☐ Passport ☐ Personally Known ☐ I D Card ☐ Other_____ ☐ I D. # _____		

223 Notary Public Record

Notarized Date/Time	Date of Document	Type of Documents	Service	Name, Phone #, address of signer	E-mail:
		_____	☐ Acknowledgment ☐ Oath/Affirmation ☐ Jurat ☐ Other _____	_____	Signature
_____	_____	_____		_____	_____

Name, Phone #, address of witness	Signature of witness	Identity	Right Thumbprint	Notary / Travel Fee
_____ _____		☐ Driver's license ☐ Credible Witness ☐ Passport ☐ Personally Known ☐ I D Card ☐ Other_____ ☐ I D. # _____		

224 Notary Public Record

Notarized Date/Time	Date of Document	Type of Documents	Service	Name, Phone #, address of signer	E-mail:
		_____	☐ Acknowledgment ☐ Oath/Affirmation ☐ Jurat ☐ Other _____	_____	Signature
_____	_____	_____		_____	_____

Name, Phone #, address of witness	Signature of witness	Identity	Right Thumbprint	Notary / Travel Fee
_____ _____		☐ Driver's license ☐ Credible Witness ☐ Passport ☐ Personally Known ☐ I D Card ☐ Other_____ ☐ I D. # _____		

225 Notary Public Record

Notarized Date/Time	Date of Document	Type of Documents	Service	Name, Phone #, address of signer	E-mail:
		_____	☐ Acknowledgment ☐ Oath/Affirmation ☐ Jurat ☐ Other _____	_____	Signature
_____	_____	_____		_____	_____

Name, Phone #, address of witness	Signature of witness	Identity	Right Thumbprint	Notary / Travel Fee
_____ _____		☐ Driver's license ☐ Credible Witness ☐ Passport ☐ Personally Known ☐ I D Card ☐ Other_____ ☐ I D. # _____		

226 Notary Public Record

Notarized Date/Time	Date of Document	Type of Documents	Service	Name, Phone #, address of signer	E-mail:
			☐ Acknowledgment ☐ Oath/Affirmation ☐ Jurat ☐ Other _____		Signature

Name, Phone #, address of witness	Signature of witness	Identity	Right Thumbprint	Notary / Travel Fee
		☐ Driver's license ☐ Credible Witness ☐ Passport ☐ Personally Known ☐ I D Card ☐ Other_____ ☐ I D. # _____		

227 Notary Public Record

Notarized Date/Time	Date of Document	Type of Documents	Service	Name, Phone #, address of signer	E-mail:
			☐ Acknowledgment ☐ Oath/Affirmation ☐ Jurat ☐ Other _____		Signature

Name, Phone #, address of witness	Signature of witness	Identity	Right Thumbprint	Notary / Travel Fee
		☐ Driver's license ☐ Credible Witness ☐ Passport ☐ Personally Known ☐ I D Card ☐ Other_____ ☐ I D. # _____		

228 Notary Public Record

Notarized Date/Time	Date of Document	Type of Documents	Service	Name, Phone #, address of signer	E-mail:
			☐ Acknowledgment ☐ Oath/Affirmation ☐ Jurat ☐ Other _____		Signature

Name, Phone #, address of witness	Signature of witness	Identity	Right Thumbprint	Notary / Travel Fee
		☐ Driver's license ☐ Credible Witness ☐ Passport ☐ Personally Known ☐ I D Card ☐ Other_____ ☐ I D. # _____		

229 Notary Public Record

Notarized Date/Time	Date of Document	Type of Documents	Service	Name, Phone #, address of signer	E-mail:
			☐ Acknowledgment ☐ Oath/Affirmation ☐ Jurat ☐ Other _____		Signature

Name, Phone #, address of witness	Signature of witness	Identity	Right Thumbprint	Notary / Travel Fee
		☐ Driver's license ☐ Credible Witness ☐ Passport ☐ Personally Known ☐ I D Card ☐ Other_____ ☐ I D. # _____		

230 Notary Public Record

Notarized Date/Time	Date of Document	Type of Documents	Service	Name, Phone #, address of signer	E-mail:
			☐ Acknowledgment ☐ Oath/Affirmation ☐ Jurat ☐ Other _____		Signature

Name, Phone #, address of witness	Signature of witness	Identity	Right Thumbprint	Notary / Travel Fee
		☐ Driver's license ☐ Credible Witness ☐ Passport ☐ Personally Known ☐ I D Card ☐ Other_____ ☐ I D. # _____		

231 Notary Public Record

Notarized Date/Time	Date of Document	Type of Documents	Service	Name, Phone #, address of signer	E-mail:
			☐ Acknowledgment ☐ Oath/Affirmation ☐ Jurat ☐ Other _____		Signature

Name, Phone #, address of witness	Signature of witness	Identity	Right Thumbprint	Notary / Travel Fee
		☐ Driver's license ☐ Credible Witness ☐ Passport ☐ Personally Known ☐ I D Card ☐ Other_____ ☐ I D. # _____		

232 Notary Public Record

Notarized Date/Time	Date of Document	Type of Documents	Service	Name, Phone #, address of signer	E-mail:
			☐ Acknowledgment ☐ Oath/Affirmation ☐ Jurat ☐ Other _____		Signature

Name, Phone #, address of witness	Signature of witness	Identity	Right Thumbprint	Notary / Travel Fee
		☐ Driver's license ☐ Credible Witness ☐ Passport ☐ Personally Known ☐ I D Card ☐ Other_____ ☐ I D. # _____		

233 Notary Public Record

Notarized Date/Time	Date of Document	Type of Documents	Service	Name, Phone #, address of signer	E-mail:
			☐ Acknowledgment ☐ Oath/Affirmation ☐ Jurat ☐ Other _____		Signature

Name, Phone #, address of witness	Signature of witness	Identity	Right Thumbprint	Notary / Travel Fee
		☐ Driver's license ☐ Credible Witness ☐ Passport ☐ Personally Known ☐ I D Card ☐ Other_____ ☐ I D. # _____		

234 Notary Public Record

Notarized Date/Time	Date of Document	Type of Documents	Service	Name, Phone #, address of signer	E-mail:
			☐ Acknowledgment ☐ Oath/Affirmation ☐ Jurat ☐ Other _____		Signature

Name, Phone #, address of witness	Signature of witness	Identity	Right Thumbprint	Notary / Travel Fee
		☐ Driver's license ☐ Credible Witness ☐ Passport ☐ Personally Known ☐ I D Card ☐ Other_____ ☐ I D. # _____		

235 Notary Public Record

Notarized Date/Time	Date of Document	Type of Documents	Service	Name, Phone #, address of signer	E-mail:
		_____	☐ Acknowledgment ☐ Oath/Affirmation ☐ Jurat ☐ Other _____	_____	Signature
_____	_____	_____		_____	_____

Name, Phone #, address of witness	Signature of witness	Identity	Right Thumbprint	Notary / Travel Fee
_____		☐ Driver's license ☐ Credible Witness ☐ Passport ☐ Personally Known ☐ I D Card ☐ Other_____ ☐ I D. # _____		

236 Notary Public Record

Notarized Date/Time	Date of Document	Type of Documents	Service	Name, Phone #, address of signer	E-mail:
		_____	☐ Acknowledgment ☐ Oath/Affirmation ☐ Jurat ☐ Other _____	_____	Signature
_____	_____	_____		_____	_____

Name, Phone #, address of witness	Signature of witness	Identity	Right Thumbprint	Notary / Travel Fee
_____		☐ Driver's license ☐ Credible Witness ☐ Passport ☐ Personally Known ☐ I D Card ☐ Other_____ ☐ I D. # _____		

237 Notary Public Record

Notarized Date/Time	Date of Document	Type of Documents	Service	Name, Phone #, address of signer	E-mail:
		_____	☐ Acknowledgment ☐ Oath/Affirmation ☐ Jurat ☐ Other _____	_____	Signature
_____	_____	_____		_____	_____

Name, Phone #, address of witness	Signature of witness	Identity	Right Thumbprint	Notary / Travel Fee
_____		☐ Driver's license ☐ Credible Witness ☐ Passport ☐ Personally Known ☐ I D Card ☐ Other_____ ☐ I D. # _____		

238 Notary Public Record

Notarized Date/Time	Date of Document	Type of Documents	Service	Name, Phone #, address of signer	E-mail:
			☐ Acknowledgment ☐ Oath/Affirmation ☐ Jurat ☐ Other _____		Signature

Name, Phone #, address of witness	Signature of witness	Identity	Right Thumbprint	Notary / Travel Fee
		☐ Driver's license ☐ Credible Witness ☐ Passport ☐ Personally Known ☐ I D Card ☐ Other_____ ☐ I D. # _____		

239 Notary Public Record

Notarized Date/Time	Date of Document	Type of Documents	Service	Name, Phone #, address of signer	E-mail:
			☐ Acknowledgment ☐ Oath/Affirmation ☐ Jurat ☐ Other _____		Signature

Name, Phone #, address of witness	Signature of witness	Identity	Right Thumbprint	Notary / Travel Fee
		☐ Driver's license ☐ Credible Witness ☐ Passport ☐ Personally Known ☐ I D Card ☐ Other_____ ☐ I D. # _____		

240 Notary Public Record

Notarized Date/Time	Date of Document	Type of Documents	Service	Name, Phone #, address of signer	E-mail:
			☐ Acknowledgment ☐ Oath/Affirmation ☐ Jurat ☐ Other _____		Signature

Name, Phone #, address of witness	Signature of witness	Identity	Right Thumbprint	Notary / Travel Fee
		☐ Driver's license ☐ Credible Witness ☐ Passport ☐ Personally Known ☐ I D Card ☐ Other_____ ☐ I D. # _____		

241 Notary Public Record

Notarized Date/Time	Date of Document	Type of Documents	Service	Name, Phone #, address of signer	E-mail:
		_____	☐ Acknowledgment ☐ Oath/Affirmation ☐ Jurat ☐ Other _____	_____	Signature
_____	_____	_____		_____	_____

Name, Phone #, address of witness	Signature of witness	Identity	Right Thumbprint	Notary / Travel Fee
_____		☐ Driver's license ☐ Credible Witness ☐ Passport ☐ Personally Known ☐ I D Card ☐ Other_____		
_____		☐ I D. # _____		

242 Notary Public Record

Notarized Date/Time	Date of Document	Type of Documents	Service	Name, Phone #, address of signer	E-mail:
		_____	☐ Acknowledgment ☐ Oath/Affirmation ☐ Jurat ☐ Other _____	_____	Signature
_____	_____	_____		_____	_____

Name, Phone #, address of witness	Signature of witness	Identity	Right Thumbprint	Notary / Travel Fee
_____		☐ Driver's license ☐ Credible Witness ☐ Passport ☐ Personally Known ☐ I D Card ☐ Other_____		
_____		☐ I D. # _____		

243 Notary Public Record

Notarized Date/Time	Date of Document	Type of Documents	Service	Name, Phone #, address of signer	E-mail:
		_____	☐ Acknowledgment ☐ Oath/Affirmation ☐ Jurat ☐ Other _____	_____	Signature
_____	_____	_____		_____	_____

Name, Phone #, address of witness	Signature of witness	Identity	Right Thumbprint	Notary / Travel Fee
_____		☐ Driver's license ☐ Credible Witness ☐ Passport ☐ Personally Known ☐ I D Card ☐ Other_____		
_____		☐ I D. # _____		

244 Notary Public Record

Notarized Date/Time	Date of Document	Type of Documents	Service	Name, Phone #, address of signer	E-mail:
			☐ Acknowledgment ☐ Oath/Affirmation ☐ Jurat ☐ Other _____		Signature

Name, Phone #, address of witness	Signature of witness	Identity	Right Thumbprint	Notary / Travel Fee
		☐ Driver's license ☐ Credible Witness ☐ Passport ☐ Personally Known ☐ I D Card ☐ Other_____ ☐ I D. # _____		

245 Notary Public Record

Notarized Date/Time	Date of Document	Type of Documents	Service	Name, Phone #, address of signer	E-mail:
			☐ Acknowledgment ☐ Oath/Affirmation ☐ Jurat ☐ Other _____		Signature

Name, Phone #, address of witness	Signature of witness	Identity	Right Thumbprint	Notary / Travel Fee
		☐ Driver's license ☐ Credible Witness ☐ Passport ☐ Personally Known ☐ I D Card ☐ Other_____ ☐ I D. # _____		

246 Notary Public Record

Notarized Date/Time	Date of Document	Type of Documents	Service	Name, Phone #, address of signer	E-mail:
			☐ Acknowledgment ☐ Oath/Affirmation ☐ Jurat ☐ Other _____		Signature

Name, Phone #, address of witness	Signature of witness	Identity	Right Thumbprint	Notary / Travel Fee
		☐ Driver's license ☐ Credible Witness ☐ Passport ☐ Personally Known ☐ I D Card ☐ Other_____ ☐ I D. # _____		

247 Notary Public Record

Notarized Date/Time	Date of Document	Type of Documents	Service	Name, Phone #, address of signer	E-mail:
			☐ Acknowledgment ☐ Oath/Affirmation ☐ Jurat ☐ Other _____		Signature

Name, Phone #, address of witness	Signature of witness	Identity	Right Thumbprint	Notary / Travel Fee
		☐ Driver's license ☐ Credible Witness ☐ Passport ☐ Personally Known ☐ I D Card ☐ Other_____ ☐ I D. # _____		

248 Notary Public Record

Notarized Date/Time	Date of Document	Type of Documents	Service	Name, Phone #, address of signer	E-mail:
			☐ Acknowledgment ☐ Oath/Affirmation ☐ Jurat ☐ Other _____		Signature

Name, Phone #, address of witness	Signature of witness	Identity	Right Thumbprint	Notary / Travel Fee
		☐ Driver's license ☐ Credible Witness ☐ Passport ☐ Personally Known ☐ I D Card ☐ Other_____ ☐ I D. # _____		

249 Notary Public Record

Notarized Date/Time	Date of Document	Type of Documents	Service	Name, Phone #, address of signer	E-mail:
			☐ Acknowledgment ☐ Oath/Affirmation ☐ Jurat ☐ Other _____		Signature

Name, Phone #, address of witness	Signature of witness	Identity	Right Thumbprint	Notary / Travel Fee
		☐ Driver's license ☐ Credible Witness ☐ Passport ☐ Personally Known ☐ I D Card ☐ Other_____ ☐ I D. # _____		

Notary Public Record

250

Notarized Date/Time	Date of Document	Type of Documents	Service	Name, Phone #, address of signer	E-mail:
_____	_____	_____	☐ Acknowledgment ☐ Oath/Affirmation ☐ Jurat ☐ Other ————	_____	Signature
_____		_____		_____	_____

Name, Phone #, address of witness	Signature of witness	Identity	Right Thumbprint	Notary / Travel Fee
_____ _____		☐ Driver's license ☐ Credible Witness ☐ Passport ☐ Personally Known ☐ I D Card ☐ Other_____ ☐ I D. # _____		

Notary Public Record

251

Notarized Date/Time	Date of Document	Type of Documents	Service	Name, Phone #, address of signer	E-mail:
_____	_____	_____	☐ Acknowledgment ☐ Oath/Affirmation ☐ Jurat ☐ Other ————	_____	Signature
_____		_____		_____	_____

Name, Phone #, address of witness	Signature of witness	Identity	Right Thumbprint	Notary / Travel Fee
_____ _____		☐ Driver's license ☐ Credible Witness ☐ Passport ☐ Personally Known ☐ I D Card ☐ Other_____ ☐ I D. # _____		

Notary Public Record

252

Notarized Date/Time	Date of Document	Type of Documents	Service	Name, Phone #, address of signer	E-mail:
_____	_____	_____	☐ Acknowledgment ☐ Oath/Affirmation ☐ Jurat ☐ Other ————	_____	Signature
_____		_____		_____	_____

Name, Phone #, address of witness	Signature of witness	Identity	Right Thumbprint	Notary / Travel Fee
_____ _____		☐ Driver's license ☐ Credible Witness ☐ Passport ☐ Personally Known ☐ I D Card ☐ Other_____ ☐ I D. # _____		

253 Notary Public Record

Notarized Date/Time	Date of Document	Type of Documents	Service	Name, Phone #, address of signer	E-mail:
			☐ Acknowledgment ☐ Oath/Affirmation ☐ Jurat ☐ Other _____		Signature

Name, Phone #, address of witness	Signature of witness	Identity	Right Thumbprint	Notary / Travel Fee
		☐ Driver's license ☐ Credible Witness ☐ Passport ☐ Personally Known ☐ I D Card ☐ Other_____ ☐ I D. # _____		

254 Notary Public Record

Notarized Date/Time	Date of Document	Type of Documents	Service	Name, Phone #, address of signer	E-mail:
			☐ Acknowledgment ☐ Oath/Affirmation ☐ Jurat ☐ Other _____		Signature

Name, Phone #, address of witness	Signature of witness	Identity	Right Thumbprint	Notary / Travel Fee
		☐ Driver's license ☐ Credible Witness ☐ Passport ☐ Personally Known ☐ I D Card ☐ Other_____ ☐ I D. # _____		

255 Notary Public Record

Notarized Date/Time	Date of Document	Type of Documents	Service	Name, Phone #, address of signer	E-mail:
			☐ Acknowledgment ☐ Oath/Affirmation ☐ Jurat ☐ Other _____		Signature

Name, Phone #, address of witness	Signature of witness	Identity	Right Thumbprint	Notary / Travel Fee
		☐ Driver's license ☐ Credible Witness ☐ Passport ☐ Personally Known ☐ I D Card ☐ Other_____ ☐ I D. # _____		

256 Notary Public Record

Notarized Date/Time	Date of Document	Type of Documents	Service	Name, Phone #, address of signer	E-mail:
			☐ Acknowledgment ☐ Oath/Affirmation ☐ Jurat ☐ Other _____		Signature

Name, Phone #, address of witness	Signature of witness	Identity	Right Thumbprint	Notary / Travel Fee
		☐ Driver's license ☐ Credible Witness ☐ Passport ☐ Personally Known ☐ I D Card ☐ Other_____ ☐ I D. # _____		

257 Notary Public Record

Notarized Date/Time	Date of Document	Type of Documents	Service	Name, Phone #, address of signer	E-mail:
			☐ Acknowledgment ☐ Oath/Affirmation ☐ Jurat ☐ Other _____		Signature

Name, Phone #, address of witness	Signature of witness	Identity	Right Thumbprint	Notary / Travel Fee
		☐ Driver's license ☐ Credible Witness ☐ Passport ☐ Personally Known ☐ I D Card ☐ Other_____ ☐ I D. # _____		

258 Notary Public Record

Notarized Date/Time	Date of Document	Type of Documents	Service	Name, Phone #, address of signer	E-mail:
			☐ Acknowledgment ☐ Oath/Affirmation ☐ Jurat ☐ Other _____		Signature

Name, Phone #, address of witness	Signature of witness	Identity	Right Thumbprint	Notary / Travel Fee
		☐ Driver's license ☐ Credible Witness ☐ Passport ☐ Personally Known ☐ I D Card ☐ Other_____ ☐ I D. # _____		

259 Notary Public Record

Notarized Date/Time	Date of Document	Type of Documents	Service	Name, Phone #, address of signer	E-mail:
		_____	☐ Acknowledgment ☐ Oath/Affirmation ☐ Jurat ☐ Other _____	_____	Signature
_____	_____	_____		_____	
_____		_____		_____	_____

Name, Phone #, address of witness	Signature of witness	Identity	Right Thumbprint	Notary / Travel Fee
_____		☐ Driver's license ☐ Credible Witness ☐ Passport ☐ Personally Known ☐ I D Card ☐ Other_____		
_____		☐ I D. # _____		

260 Notary Public Record

Notarized Date/Time	Date of Document	Type of Documents	Service	Name, Phone #, address of signer	E-mail:
		_____	☐ Acknowledgment ☐ Oath/Affirmation ☐ Jurat ☐ Other _____	_____	Signature
_____	_____	_____		_____	
_____		_____		_____	_____

Name, Phone #, address of witness	Signature of witness	Identity	Right Thumbprint	Notary / Travel Fee
_____		☐ Driver's license ☐ Credible Witness ☐ Passport ☐ Personally Known ☐ I D Card ☐ Other_____		
_____		☐ I D. # _____		

261 Notary Public Record

Notarized Date/Time	Date of Document	Type of Documents	Service	Name, Phone #, address of signer	E-mail:
		_____	☐ Acknowledgment ☐ Oath/Affirmation ☐ Jurat ☐ Other _____	_____	Signature
_____	_____	_____		_____	
_____		_____		_____	_____

Name, Phone #, address of witness	Signature of witness	Identity	Right Thumbprint	Notary / Travel Fee
_____		☐ Driver's license ☐ Credible Witness ☐ Passport ☐ Personally Known ☐ I D Card ☐ Other_____		
_____		☐ I D. # _____		

Notary Public Record

262

Notarized Date/Time	Date of Document	Type of Documents	Service	Name, Phone #, address of signer	E-mail:
			☐ Acknowledgment ☐ Oath/Affirmation ☐ Jurat ☐ Other _____		Signature

Name, Phone #, address of witness	Signature of witness	Identity	Right Thumbprint	Notary / Travel Fee
		☐ Driver's license ☐ Credible Witness ☐ Passport ☐ Personally Known ☐ I D Card ☐ Other_____ ☐ I D. # _____		

Notary Public Record

263

Notarized Date/Time	Date of Document	Type of Documents	Service	Name, Phone #, address of signer	E-mail:
			☐ Acknowledgment ☐ Oath/Affirmation ☐ Jurat ☐ Other _____		Signature

Name, Phone #, address of witness	Signature of witness	Identity	Right Thumbprint	Notary / Travel Fee
		☐ Driver's license ☐ Credible Witness ☐ Passport ☐ Personally Known ☐ I D Card ☐ Other_____ ☐ I D. # _____		

Notary Public Record

264

Notarized Date/Time	Date of Document	Type of Documents	Service	Name, Phone #, address of signer	E-mail:
			☐ Acknowledgment ☐ Oath/Affirmation ☐ Jurat ☐ Other _____		Signature

Name, Phone #, address of witness	Signature of witness	Identity	Right Thumbprint	Notary / Travel Fee
		☐ Driver's license ☐ Credible Witness ☐ Passport ☐ Personally Known ☐ I D Card ☐ Other_____ ☐ I D. # _____		

265 Notary Public Record

Notarized Date/Time	Date of Document	Type of Documents	Service	Name, Phone #, address of signer	E-mail:
			☐ Acknowledgment ☐ Oath/Affirmation ☐ Jurat ☐ Other _____		Signature

Name, Phone #, address of witness	Signature of witness	Identity	Right Thumbprint	Notary / Travel Fee
		☐ Driver's license ☐ Credible Witness ☐ Passport ☐ Personally Known ☐ I D Card ☐ Other_____ ☐ I D. # _____		

266 Notary Public Record

Notarized Date/Time	Date of Document	Type of Documents	Service	Name, Phone #, address of signer	E-mail:
			☐ Acknowledgment ☐ Oath/Affirmation ☐ Jurat ☐ Other _____		Signature

Name, Phone #, address of witness	Signature of witness	Identity	Right Thumbprint	Notary / Travel Fee
		☐ Driver's license ☐ Credible Witness ☐ Passport ☐ Personally Known ☐ I D Card ☐ Other_____ ☐ I D. # _____		

267 Notary Public Record

Notarized Date/Time	Date of Document	Type of Documents	Service	Name, Phone #, address of signer	E-mail:
			☐ Acknowledgment ☐ Oath/Affirmation ☐ Jurat ☐ Other _____		Signature

Name, Phone #, address of witness	Signature of witness	Identity	Right Thumbprint	Notary / Travel Fee
		☐ Driver's license ☐ Credible Witness ☐ Passport ☐ Personally Known ☐ I D Card ☐ Other_____ ☐ I D. # _____		

Notary Public Record

268

Notarized Date/Time	Date of Document	Type of Documents	Service	Name, Phone #, address of signer	E-mail:
			☐ Acknowledgment ☐ Oath/Affirmation ☐ Jurat ☐ Other _____		Signature

Name, Phone #, address of witness	Signature of witness	Identity	Right Thumbprint	Notary / Travel Fee
		☐ Driver's license ☐ Credible Witness ☐ Passport ☐ Personally Known ☐ I D Card ☐ Other_____ ☐ I D. # _____		

Notary Public Record

269

Notarized Date/Time	Date of Document	Type of Documents	Service	Name, Phone #, address of signer	E-mail:
			☐ Acknowledgment ☐ Oath/Affirmation ☐ Jurat ☐ Other _____		Signature

Name, Phone #, address of witness	Signature of witness	Identity	Right Thumbprint	Notary / Travel Fee
		☐ Driver's license ☐ Credible Witness ☐ Passport ☐ Personally Known ☐ I D Card ☐ Other_____ ☐ I D. # _____		

Notary Public Record

270

Notarized Date/Time	Date of Document	Type of Documents	Service	Name, Phone #, address of signer	E-mail:
			☐ Acknowledgment ☐ Oath/Affirmation ☐ Jurat ☐ Other _____		Signature

Name, Phone #, address of witness	Signature of witness	Identity	Right Thumbprint	Notary / Travel Fee
		☐ Driver's license ☐ Credible Witness ☐ Passport ☐ Personally Known ☐ I D Card ☐ Other_____ ☐ I D. # _____		

271 Notary Public Record

Notarized Date/Time	Date of Document	Type of Documents	Service	Name, Phone #, address of signer	E-mail:
		_____	☐ Acknowledgment ☐ Oath/Affirmation ☐ Jurat ☐ Other _____	_____	Signature
_____	_____	_____		_____	
		_____		_____	_____

Name, Phone #, address of witness	Signature of witness	Identity	Right Thumbprint	Notary / Travel Fee
		☐ Driver's license ☐ Credible Witness ☐ Passport ☐ Personally Known ☐ ID Card ☐ Other_____ ☐ ID. # _____		

272 Notary Public Record

Notarized Date/Time	Date of Document	Type of Documents	Service	Name, Phone #, address of signer	E-mail:
		_____	☐ Acknowledgment ☐ Oath/Affirmation ☐ Jurat ☐ Other _____	_____	Signature
_____	_____	_____		_____	
		_____		_____	_____

Name, Phone #, address of witness	Signature of witness	Identity	Right Thumbprint	Notary / Travel Fee
		☐ Driver's license ☐ Credible Witness ☐ Passport ☐ Personally Known ☐ ID Card ☐ Other_____ ☐ ID. # _____		

273 Notary Public Record

Notarized Date/Time	Date of Document	Type of Documents	Service	Name, Phone #, address of signer	E-mail:
		_____	☐ Acknowledgment ☐ Oath/Affirmation ☐ Jurat ☐ Other _____	_____	Signature
_____	_____	_____		_____	
		_____		_____	_____

Name, Phone #, address of witness	Signature of witness	Identity	Right Thumbprint	Notary / Travel Fee
		☐ Driver's license ☐ Credible Witness ☐ Passport ☐ Personally Known ☐ ID Card ☐ Other_____ ☐ ID. # _____		

274

Notary Public Record

Notarized Date/Time	Date of Document	Type of Documents	Service	Name, Phone #, address of signer	E-mail:
			☐ Acknowledgment ☐ Oath/Affirmation ☐ Jurat ☐ Other _____		Signature

Name, Phone #, address of witness	Signature of witness	Identity	Right Thumbprint	Notary / Travel Fee
		☐ Driver's license ☐ Credible Witness ☐ Passport ☐ Personally Known ☐ I D Card ☐ Other_____ ☐ I D. # _____		

275

Notary Public Record

Notarized Date/Time	Date of Document	Type of Documents	Service	Name, Phone #, address of signer	E-mail:
			☐ Acknowledgment ☐ Oath/Affirmation ☐ Jurat ☐ Other _____		Signature

Name, Phone #, address of witness	Signature of witness	Identity	Right Thumbprint	Notary / Travel Fee
		☐ Driver's license ☐ Credible Witness ☐ Passport ☐ Personally Known ☐ I D Card ☐ Other_____ ☐ I D. # _____		

276

Notary Public Record

Notarized Date/Time	Date of Document	Type of Documents	Service	Name, Phone #, address of signer	E-mail:
			☐ Acknowledgment ☐ Oath/Affirmation ☐ Jurat ☐ Other _____		Signature

Name, Phone #, address of witness	Signature of witness	Identity	Right Thumbprint	Notary / Travel Fee
		☐ Driver's license ☐ Credible Witness ☐ Passport ☐ Personally Known ☐ I D Card ☐ Other_____ ☐ I D. # _____		

277

Notary Public Record

Notarized Date/Time	Date of Document	Type of Documents	Service	Name, Phone #, address of signer	E-mail:
		_____	☐ Acknowledgment ☐ Oath/Affirmation ☐ Jurat ☐ Other _____	_____	Signature
_____	_____	_____		_____	_____

Name, Phone #, address of witness	Signature of witness	Identity	Right Thumbprint	Notary / Travel Fee
_____		☐ Driver's license ☐ Credible Witness ☐ Passport ☐ Personally Known ☐ I D Card ☐ Other_____ ☐ I D. # _____		

278

Notary Public Record

Notarized Date/Time	Date of Document	Type of Documents	Service	Name, Phone #, address of signer	E-mail:
		_____	☐ Acknowledgment ☐ Oath/Affirmation ☐ Jurat ☐ Other _____	_____	Signature
_____	_____	_____		_____	_____

Name, Phone #, address of witness	Signature of witness	Identity	Right Thumbprint	Notary / Travel Fee
_____		☐ Driver's license ☐ Credible Witness ☐ Passport ☐ Personally Known ☐ I D Card ☐ Other_____ ☐ I D. # _____		

279

Notary Public Record

Notarized Date/Time	Date of Document	Type of Documents	Service	Name, Phone #, address of signer	E-mail:
		_____	☐ Acknowledgment ☐ Oath/Affirmation ☐ Jurat ☐ Other _____	_____	Signature
_____	_____	_____		_____	_____

Name, Phone #, address of witness	Signature of witness	Identity	Right Thumbprint	Notary / Travel Fee
_____		☐ Driver's license ☐ Credible Witness ☐ Passport ☐ Personally Known ☐ I D Card ☐ Other_____ ☐ I D. # _____		

280 Notary Public Record

Notarized Date/Time	Date of Document	Type of Documents	Service	Name, Phone #, address of signer	E-mail:
			☐ Acknowledgment ☐ Oath/Affirmation ☐ Jurat ☐ Other ————		Signature

Name, Phone #, address of witness	Signature of witness	Identity	Right Thumbprint	Notary / Travel Fee
		☐ Driver's license ☐ Credible Witness ☐ Passport ☐ Personally Known ☐ I D Card ☐ Other_____ ☐ I D. # _____		

281 Notary Public Record

Notarized Date/Time	Date of Document	Type of Documents	Service	Name, Phone #, address of signer	E-mail:
			☐ Acknowledgment ☐ Oath/Affirmation ☐ Jurat ☐ Other ————		Signature

Name, Phone #, address of witness	Signature of witness	Identity	Right Thumbprint	Notary / Travel Fee
		☐ Driver's license ☐ Credible Witness ☐ Passport ☐ Personally Known ☐ I D Card ☐ Other_____ ☐ I D. # _____		

282 Notary Public Record

Notarized Date/Time	Date of Document	Type of Documents	Service	Name, Phone #, address of signer	E-mail:
			☐ Acknowledgment ☐ Oath/Affirmation ☐ Jurat ☐ Other ————		Signature

Name, Phone #, address of witness	Signature of witness	Identity	Right Thumbprint	Notary / Travel Fee
		☐ Driver's license ☐ Credible Witness ☐ Passport ☐ Personally Known ☐ I D Card ☐ Other_____ ☐ I D. # _____		

283 Notary Public Record

Notarized Date/Time	Date of Document	Type of Documents	Service	Name, Phone #, address of signer	E-mail:
			☐ Acknowledgment ☐ Oath/Affirmation ☐ Jurat ☐ Other ————		Signature

Name, Phone #, address of witness	Signature of witness	Identity	Right Thumbprint	Notary / Travel Fee
		☐ Driver's license ☐ Credible Witness ☐ Passport ☐ Personally Known ☐ I D Card ☐ Other_____ ☐ I D. #_____		

284 Notary Public Record

Notarized Date/Time	Date of Document	Type of Documents	Service	Name, Phone #, address of signer	E-mail:
			☐ Acknowledgment ☐ Oath/Affirmation ☐ Jurat ☐ Other ————		Signature

Name, Phone #, address of witness	Signature of witness	Identity	Right Thumbprint	Notary / Travel Fee
		☐ Driver's license ☐ Credible Witness ☐ Passport ☐ Personally Known ☐ I D Card ☐ Other_____ ☐ I D. #_____		

285 Notary Public Record

Notarized Date/Time	Date of Document	Type of Documents	Service	Name, Phone #, address of signer	E-mail:
			☐ Acknowledgment ☐ Oath/Affirmation ☐ Jurat ☐ Other ————		Signature

Name, Phone #, address of witness	Signature of witness	Identity	Right Thumbprint	Notary / Travel Fee
		☐ Driver's license ☐ Credible Witness ☐ Passport ☐ Personally Known ☐ I D Card ☐ Other_____ ☐ I D. #_____		

286 Notary Public Record

Notarized Date/Time	Date of Document	Type of Documents	Service	Name, Phone #, address of signer	E-mail:
			☐ Acknowledgment ☐ Oath/Affirmation ☐ Jurat ☐ Other ————		Signature

Name, Phone #, address of witness	Signature of witness	Identity	Right Thumbprint	Notary / Travel Fee
		☐ Driver's license ☐ Credible Witness ☐ Passport ☐ Personally Known ☐ I D Card ☐ Other_____ ☐ I D. #_____		

287 Notary Public Record

Notarized Date/Time	Date of Document	Type of Documents	Service	Name, Phone #, address of signer	E-mail:
			☐ Acknowledgment ☐ Oath/Affirmation ☐ Jurat ☐ Other ————		Signature

Name, Phone #, address of witness	Signature of witness	Identity	Right Thumbprint	Notary / Travel Fee
		☐ Driver's license ☐ Credible Witness ☐ Passport ☐ Personally Known ☐ I D Card ☐ Other_____ ☐ I D. #_____		

288 Notary Public Record

Notarized Date/Time	Date of Document	Type of Documents	Service	Name, Phone #, address of signer	E-mail:
			☐ Acknowledgment ☐ Oath/Affirmation ☐ Jurat ☐ Other ————		Signature

Name, Phone #, address of witness	Signature of witness	Identity	Right Thumbprint	Notary / Travel Fee
		☐ Driver's license ☐ Credible Witness ☐ Passport ☐ Personally Known ☐ I D Card ☐ Other_____ ☐ I D. #_____		

289 Notary Public Record

Notarized Date/Time	Date of Document	Type of Documents	Service	Name, Phone #, address of signer	E-mail:
			☐ Acknowledgment ☐ Oath/Affirmation ☐ Jurat ☐ Other _____		Signature

Name, Phone #, address of witness	Signature of witness	Identity	Right Thumbprint	Notary / Travel Fee
		☐ Driver's license ☐ Credible Witness ☐ Passport ☐ Personally Known ☐ I D Card ☐ Other_____ ☐ I D. # _____		

290 Notary Public Record

Notarized Date/Time	Date of Document	Type of Documents	Service	Name, Phone #, address of signer	E-mail:
			☐ Acknowledgment ☐ Oath/Affirmation ☐ Jurat ☐ Other _____		Signature

Name, Phone #, address of witness	Signature of witness	Identity	Right Thumbprint	Notary / Travel Fee
		☐ Driver's license ☐ Credible Witness ☐ Passport ☐ Personally Known ☐ I D Card ☐ Other_____ ☐ I D. # _____		

291 Notary Public Record

Notarized Date/Time	Date of Document	Type of Documents	Service	Name, Phone #, address of signer	E-mail:
			☐ Acknowledgment ☐ Oath/Affirmation ☐ Jurat ☐ Other _____		Signature

Name, Phone #, address of witness	Signature of witness	Identity	Right Thumbprint	Notary / Travel Fee
		☐ Driver's license ☐ Credible Witness ☐ Passport ☐ Personally Known ☐ I D Card ☐ Other_____ ☐ I D. # _____		

292   *Notary Public Record*

Notarized Date/Time	Date of Document	Type of Documents	Service	Name, Phone #, address of signer	E-mail:
			☐ Acknowledgment ☐ Oath/Affirmation ☐ Jurat ☐ Other _____		Signature

Name, Phone #, address of witness	Signature of witness	Identity	Right Thumbprint	Notary / Travel Fee
		☐ Driver's license ☐ Credible Witness ☐ Passport ☐ Personally Known ☐ I D Card ☐ Other_____ ☐ I D. # _____		

293   *Notary Public Record*

Notarized Date/Time	Date of Document	Type of Documents	Service	Name, Phone #, address of signer	E-mail:
			☐ Acknowledgment ☐ Oath/Affirmation ☐ Jurat ☐ Other _____		Signature

Name, Phone #, address of witness	Signature of witness	Identity	Right Thumbprint	Notary / Travel Fee
		☐ Driver's license ☐ Credible Witness ☐ Passport ☐ Personally Known ☐ I D Card ☐ Other_____ ☐ I D. # _____		

294   *Notary Public Record*

Notarized Date/Time	Date of Document	Type of Documents	Service	Name, Phone #, address of signer	E-mail:
			☐ Acknowledgment ☐ Oath/Affirmation ☐ Jurat ☐ Other _____		Signature

Name, Phone #, address of witness	Signature of witness	Identity	Right Thumbprint	Notary / Travel Fee
		☐ Driver's license ☐ Credible Witness ☐ Passport ☐ Personally Known ☐ I D Card ☐ Other_____ ☐ I D. # _____		

295

Notary Public Record

Notarized Date/Time	Date of Document	Type of Documents	Service	Name, Phone #, address of signer	E-mail:
			☐ Acknowledgment ☐ Oath/Affirmation ☐ Jurat ☐ Other _____		Signature

Name, Phone #, address of witness	Signature of witness	Identity	Right Thumbprint	Notary / Travel Fee
		☐ Driver's license ☐ Credible Witness ☐ Passport ☐ Personally Known ☐ I D Card ☐ Other_____ ☐ I D. # _____		

296

Notary Public Record

Notarized Date/Time	Date of Document	Type of Documents	Service	Name, Phone #, address of signer	E-mail:
			☐ Acknowledgment ☐ Oath/Affirmation ☐ Jurat ☐ Other _____		Signature

Name, Phone #, address of witness	Signature of witness	Identity	Right Thumbprint	Notary / Travel Fee
		☐ Driver's license ☐ Credible Witness ☐ Passport ☐ Personally Known ☐ I D Card ☐ Other_____ ☐ I D. # _____		

297

Notary Public Record

Notarized Date/Time	Date of Document	Type of Documents	Service	Name, Phone #, address of signer	E-mail:
			☐ Acknowledgment ☐ Oath/Affirmation ☐ Jurat ☐ Other _____		Signature

Name, Phone #, address of witness	Signature of witness	Identity	Right Thumbprint	Notary / Travel Fee
		☐ Driver's license ☐ Credible Witness ☐ Passport ☐ Personally Known ☐ I D Card ☐ Other_____ ☐ I D. # _____		

Notary Public Record

298

Notarized Date/Time	Date of Document	Type of Documents	Service	Name, Phone #, address of signer	E-mail:
			☐ Acknowledgment ☐ Oath/Affirmation ☐ Jurat ☐ Other _____		Signature

Name, Phone #, address of witness	Signature of witness	Identity	Right Thumbprint	Notary / Travel Fee
		☐ Driver's license ☐ Credible Witness ☐ Passport ☐ Personally Known ☐ I D Card ☐ Other_____ ☐ I D. # _____		

Notary Public Record

299

Notarized Date/Time	Date of Document	Type of Documents	Service	Name, Phone #, address of signer	E-mail:
			☐ Acknowledgment ☐ Oath/Affirmation ☐ Jurat ☐ Other _____		Signature

Name, Phone #, address of witness	Signature of witness	Identity	Right Thumbprint	Notary / Travel Fee
		☐ Driver's license ☐ Credible Witness ☐ Passport ☐ Personally Known ☐ I D Card ☐ Other_____ ☐ I D. # _____		

Notary Public Record

300

Notarized Date/Time	Date of Document	Type of Documents	Service	Name, Phone #, address of signer	E-mail:
			☐ Acknowledgment ☐ Oath/Affirmation ☐ Jurat ☐ Other _____		Signature

Name, Phone #, address of witness	Signature of witness	Identity	Right Thumbprint	Notary / Travel Fee
		☐ Driver's license ☐ Credible Witness ☐ Passport ☐ Personally Known ☐ I D Card ☐ Other_____ ☐ I D. # _____		

301 Notary Public Record

Notarized Date/Time	Date of Document	Type of Documents	Service	Name, Phone #, address of signer	E-mail:
		_____	☐ Acknowledgment ☐ Oath/Affirmation ☐ Jurat ☐ Other _____	_____	Signature
_____	_____	_____		_____	_____

Name, Phone #, address of witness	Signature of witness	Identity	Right Thumbprint	Notary / Travel Fee
_____ _____		☐ Driver's license ☐ Credible Witness ☐ Passport ☐ Personally Known ☐ I D Card ☐ Other_____ ☐ I D. # _____		

302 Notary Public Record

Notarized Date/Time	Date of Document	Type of Documents	Service	Name, Phone #, address of signer	E-mail:
		_____	☐ Acknowledgment ☐ Oath/Affirmation ☐ Jurat ☐ Other _____	_____	Signature
_____	_____	_____		_____	_____

Name, Phone #, address of witness	Signature of witness	Identity	Right Thumbprint	Notary / Travel Fee
_____ _____		☐ Driver's license ☐ Credible Witness ☐ Passport ☐ Personally Known ☐ I D Card ☐ Other_____ ☐ I D. # _____		

303 Notary Public Record

Notarized Date/Time	Date of Document	Type of Documents	Service	Name, Phone #, address of signer	E-mail:
		_____	☐ Acknowledgment ☐ Oath/Affirmation ☐ Jurat ☐ Other _____	_____	Signature
_____	_____	_____		_____	_____

Name, Phone #, address of witness	Signature of witness	Identity	Right Thumbprint	Notary / Travel Fee
_____ _____		☐ Driver's license ☐ Credible Witness ☐ Passport ☐ Personally Known ☐ I D Card ☐ Other_____ ☐ I D. # _____		

304 Notary Public Record

Notarized Date/Time	Date of Document	Type of Documents	Service	Name, Phone #, address of signer	E-mail:
			☐ Acknowledgment ☐ Oath/Affirmation ☐ Jurat ☐ Other _____		Signature

Name, Phone #, address of witness	Signature of witness	Identity	Right Thumbprint	Notary / Travel Fee
		☐ Driver's license ☐ Credible Witness ☐ Passport ☐ Personally Known ☐ I D Card ☐ Other_____ ☐ I D. # _____		

305 Notary Public Record

Notarized Date/Time	Date of Document	Type of Documents	Service	Name, Phone #, address of signer	E-mail:
			☐ Acknowledgment ☐ Oath/Affirmation ☐ Jurat ☐ Other _____		Signature

Name, Phone #, address of witness	Signature of witness	Identity	Right Thumbprint	Notary / Travel Fee
		☐ Driver's license ☐ Credible Witness ☐ Passport ☐ Personally Known ☐ I D Card ☐ Other_____ ☐ I D. # _____		

306 Notary Public Record

Notarized Date/Time	Date of Document	Type of Documents	Service	Name, Phone #, address of signer	E-mail:
			☐ Acknowledgment ☐ Oath/Affirmation ☐ Jurat ☐ Other _____		Signature

Name, Phone #, address of witness	Signature of witness	Identity	Right Thumbprint	Notary / Travel Fee
		☐ Driver's license ☐ Credible Witness ☐ Passport ☐ Personally Known ☐ I D Card ☐ Other_____ ☐ I D. # _____		

307 Notary Public Record

Notarized Date/Time	Date of Document	Type of Documents	Service	Name, Phone #, address of signer	E-mail:
		_____	☐ Acknowledgment ☐ Oath/Affirmation ☐ Jurat ☐ Other _____	_____	Signature
_____	_____	_____		_____	_____

Name, Phone #, address of witness	Signature of witness	Identity	Right Thumbprint	Notary / Travel Fee
		☐ Driver's license ☐ Credible Witness ☐ Passport ☐ Personally Known ☐ I D Card ☐ Other_____ ☐ I D. # _____		

308 Notary Public Record

Notarized Date/Time	Date of Document	Type of Documents	Service	Name, Phone #, address of signer	E-mail:
		_____	☐ Acknowledgment ☐ Oath/Affirmation ☐ Jurat ☐ Other _____	_____	Signature
_____	_____	_____		_____	_____

Name, Phone #, address of witness	Signature of witness	Identity	Right Thumbprint	Notary / Travel Fee
		☐ Driver's license ☐ Credible Witness ☐ Passport ☐ Personally Known ☐ I D Card ☐ Other_____ ☐ I D. # _____		

309 Notary Public Record

Notarized Date/Time	Date of Document	Type of Documents	Service	Name, Phone #, address of signer	E-mail:
		_____	☐ Acknowledgment ☐ Oath/Affirmation ☐ Jurat ☐ Other _____	_____	Signature
_____	_____	_____		_____	_____

Name, Phone #, address of witness	Signature of witness	Identity	Right Thumbprint	Notary / Travel Fee
		☐ Driver's license ☐ Credible Witness ☐ Passport ☐ Personally Known ☐ I D Card ☐ Other_____ ☐ I D. # _____		

Notary Public Record

310

Notarized Date/Time	Date of Document	Type of Documents	Service	Name, Phone #, address of signer	E-mail:
			☐ Acknowledgment ☐ Oath/Affirmation ☐ Jurat ☐ Other _____		Signature

Name, Phone #, address of witness	Signature of witness	Identity	Right Thumbprint	Notary / Travel Fee
		☐ Driver's license ☐ Credible Witness ☐ Passport ☐ Personally Known ☐ I D Card ☐ Other_____ ☐ I D. # _____		

Notary Public Record

311

Notarized Date/Time	Date of Document	Type of Documents	Service	Name, Phone #, address of signer	E-mail:
			☐ Acknowledgment ☐ Oath/Affirmation ☐ Jurat ☐ Other _____		Signature

Name, Phone #, address of witness	Signature of witness	Identity	Right Thumbprint	Notary / Travel Fee
		☐ Driver's license ☐ Credible Witness ☐ Passport ☐ Personally Known ☐ I D Card ☐ Other_____ ☐ I D. # _____		

Notary Public Record

312

Notarized Date/Time	Date of Document	Type of Documents	Service	Name, Phone #, address of signer	E-mail:
			☐ Acknowledgment ☐ Oath/Affirmation ☐ Jurat ☐ Other _____		Signature

Name, Phone #, address of witness	Signature of witness	Identity	Right Thumbprint	Notary / Travel Fee
		☐ Driver's license ☐ Credible Witness ☐ Passport ☐ Personally Known ☐ I D Card ☐ Other_____ ☐ I D. # _____		

Made in the USA
Coppell, TX
12 November 2022

86265346R00063